MASTER HMO'S ,
CHANGE YOUR L.
FOREVER

MORE 101 QUESTIONS AND ANSWERS RELATING TO HMOs

By CJ Haliburton, the leading writer, trainer and authority on how to multi-let property

HMO Daddy
14 Walsall Road
Wednesbury
West Midlands
WS10 9JL

Print Edition
British Library Cataloguing in Publication Data.
A catalogue record for this book is available from the British Library.
Cover design and formatting by Oxford Literary Consultancy

MASTER HMO'S TODAY,
CHANGE YOUR LIFE
FOREVER

CONTENTS

INTRODUCTION 7

ACKNOWLEDGEMENT 8

PREFACE 9

I WANT TO HEAR FROM YOU 10

CHAPTER 1: ABOUT HMO DADDY 13

CHAPTER 2: HOW TO GET STARTED 33

CHAPTER 3: TENANT ISSUES 47

CHAPTER 4: LETTING TO THE UNEMPLOYED AND HOMELESS 63

CHAPTER 5: UTILITIES 79

CHAPTER 6: HMO ISSUES 89

CHAPTER 7: PROSECUTING LANDLORDS 117

CHAPTER 8: FUNDING & SOURCING PROPERTIES 126

BOOKS 140

MANUALS 146

COURSES 149

MENTORSHIPS 155

MASTER HMO'S TODAY,
CHANGE YOUR LIFE
FOREVER

WARNING

Jim Haliburton, known as the HMO Daddy, is not a lawyer or financial advisor, nor does the following represent legal or financial advice. If such advice is needed then the reader should seek professional guidance from qualified experts with appropriate public liability insurance. The following information is given to the best of Jim Haliburton's knowledge and is provided for educational purposes only. It is the reader's responsibility to obtain their own professional advice.

FREE UPDATE

This is the first edition of the book, which no doubt has mistakes which are all down to me.

If you would like the next corrected and maybe updated or revised edition then complete your details below along with your receipt and I will send you a downloadable copy of the next edition FREE OF CHARGE with no obligation.

If you have anything you wish to contribute, questions, or comments to make, please add below or send us a separate email.

_____

_____

_____

Name:

_____

Email address:

_____

How did you purchase your original copy of the book?

_____

Your details will be added to my database. If you do not wish to be entered, please put a cross in the box ☐

EMAIL WITH Λ COPY OF YOUR RECEIPT TO:
JIM@HMODADDY.COM

INTRODUCTION

Hi, I'm Jim Haliburton, also known as the HMO Daddy, as I have acquired over 140 HMOs and 30 single lets. I have more than 900 tenants and am still acquiring property. I don't say this to boast, but to show my experience. One of my passions is running training courses teaching people about HMOs and I have written many leading books and manuals on the subject. I just love sharing my experience. I was a college lecturer and I excel in sharing my passion and knowledge. The success of those I have taught proves the difference I can make to your property journey. (See 'Courses and Products' section, at back of this book).

Welcome to my first edition of 'More 101 Questions and Answers on HMOs', a sequel to '101 Question and Answers for HMO Landlords'.

If there is something you require explaining in more depth, please do not hesitate to contact a member of my team at HMO Daddy and they will be happy to help.

I sincerely hope you find the answers you are looking for in this book and that you gain extra knowledge.

Enjoy

C.J. Haliburton

June 2017

ACKNOWLEDGEMENT

I would like to thank all the HMO landlords and the people who are thinking about getting into the industry for their questions because this has made this book easy for me to write. All I had to do was ask my assistants, Rachel Neal and Toni Neal, to pull out all of the questions I have been asked since my previous book '101 Questions & Answers relating to HMOs'. They helped to categorise them, and when they reached 101 we printed them and published this book. I would like to thank Rachel Neal and Toni Neal for typing up the manuscript.

I have found certain topics keep being repeated for which there is no simple quick answer, so I have recently covered these in my book 'Top Twelve Current Issues For HMO Landlords', available from www.hmodaddy.com.

Can I also thank Sam Maddrell, Clive Pickering, Paul Charles, Elizabeth Collins and others for proofreading 'More 101 Questions and Answers on HMOs', as well as Claire Williams for her editing and suggestions. Any errors are entirely down to me.

PREFACE

I not only want to answer readers questions, but also provide an insight into the topics asked. There are plenty of bland sites out there which give information. What I find landlords want is what to make of the facts: how much importance to attach to certain things or the value thereof. I have to be careful with what I say as I do not want people accusing me of inciting people to break the law or creating dissention.

The legislation aimed at the HMO property market is over 90% unnecessary and very badly or vaguely drafted, not based on any risk analysis but mainly a wish to control and restrict HMOs. The law is selectively enforced and mostly ignored. The reason the law is mainly ignored is often that those whose duty it is to enforce the law recognise this and wish to encourage the provision of housing so are disinclined to be over-officious; also, mostly because they lack the resources. There are plenty of people who for a salary will enthusiastically enforce pointless rules, criminalise landlords and incur them in pointless expense.

I hope my answers help you, and please keep your questions coming, as I enjoy helping you.

I WANT TO HEAR FROM YOU

As a reader of the first edition of 'More 101 Questions and Answers for HMO Landlords', you are the most important critic and commentator. I value your opinion and comments. I want to know what else you would like me to include in the book, what you disagree with, and any other words of wisdom you wish me to share.

I would like feedback from you, my readers, both positive and negative. Any improvements I can incorporate to help other landlords through the maze of being an HMO landlord will be gratefully received and I am sure attract the thanks of landlords I pass them onto.

I welcome your comments and you can email or write to me to let me know what you did or didn't like about my book, as well as what I can do to make it better or what other information or service I can provide.

I also provide training courses on all aspects of the business, which you can find out about on my website www.hmodaddy.com.

When you write to me, please include your name, email address, home address and phone number. I assure you, I will value and review all of your comments. Above all, please keep your questions coming – I have nearly enough questions for the next version of this book!

Jim Haliburton

Email: jim@hmodaddy.com

Website: www.hmodaddy.com

Mail: Jim Haliburton
                  14 Walsall Road
                  Wednesbury
                  WS10 9JL

CHAPTER 1
ABOUT HMO DADDY

Previously, I kept away from talking about myself and my motivation, as I thought it would be nothing more than a distraction to those on their HMO landlord journey. From experience, most of those who want to know about me or knock me never go on to be HMO landlords – it is the opposite, the death knell. Those who ask why I do it are ones I can bet never do anything. The ones who do go on to be HMO landlords usually show little interest in me as a person, just what I know. However, I have reluctantly bowed to the clamour and shared the following.

1. **Question:** I have heard a lot of bad things said about you. How do you react to this?

   Answer: Let me compare my work to the bank manager who came to see me in late 2015. He was quite open that the bank had made bad lending decisions in lending to me and others to buy property. Now the bank either wanted its loan back or they would impose penal rates of interest; further, they would use every device it could to do so. Even though they had lent at a particular rate and for a twenty-year term, they felt they could now ignore this. If I did not renegotiate the deal again, they would foreclose on the properties, even though I was paying the mortgage and had already been forced to agree to a higher interest rate. Even worse, they would then sell the loan to an American bank who would look to make at least 20% return from their investment. If I felt my UK lender had no conscience, their overseas equivalent would be so much more ruthless! On that cheery note he left. I never had the opportunity to ask him how he liked his job in destroying businesses for profit. However, given my many years of dealing with a rogues' gallery of dodgy tenants and builders, housing officials with their pointless and often harmful standards, local councillors and planners who obstruct development, I knew it would never be their fault. After all, if they felt it was wrong, I doubt they would put up with their job for long!

I still remember, decades ago, sitting next to a bright but clearly depressed young lady on a holiday flight. She was telling me about her work as an IT consultant. She explained her job was to computerise the Revenue. She had been working on it for over two years and it would take years for it to be approved. I am not an expert on such matters, but even I knew that computer systems needed updating about every two years or so. I pointed out the system would need replacing before it had been installed and she sighed and agreed. Her distress spoke volumes! She felt trapped in her pointless job. I did not feel it was appropriate in the circumstances to point out that life is too short to waste by spending your best years doing nothing of value.

Equally, how would I feel devoting my existence to the police force where the object is to convict regardless of the merits or evidence? Or to a hollow existence in sales, trying to convince despairing wage slaves to squander their meagre earnings on the latest fripperies, regardless of need or affordability? I could go on... Maybe being what many consider to be an exploitive landlord is not such a bad thing. Let the impotent keyboard warriors on Facebook rage and rant about my sins; I'll be too busy earning good profits by providing safe, comfortable, flexible, short-term affordable accommodation at a fraction of the cost of the bloated, inefficient social sector.

2. **Question:** Jim, how did you start out?

Answer: I remember it well; it was a lovely sunny day in June 1991, the birds were singing, the trees were lush and green. I was standing outside an end-terrace house that I was considering buying to turn into my first HMO. It was situated in a small town near Birmingham called Wednesbury. The problem was my job situation. I was just over broke, like so many other people. I had little scope to increase my income as a lecturer, I did not have enough money for the lifestyle I wanted and everything I earned was spent on bills. My wife and I could only just afford a couple of budget holidays a year. Although relatively comfortable, I wanted more - preferably financial independence. So there I was, looking at this property, which was an end of terrace built about 1900. It was not in the best condition and I was wondering would this do for letting to students. I was with Angie, the college accommodation officer, who I'd had to bribe with the offer of a free expensive lunch to view the property and advise me as to its suitability for letting to students. However, she kept going on about wanting lunch, while I wanted to talk about the property.

Now the hard bit – would the property be suitable for students? If so, how should I go about preparing it for them? I only lectured students, I didn't know what they wanted in the way of accommodation, nor did I know anything about the business of being a landlord.

Nowadays, readers, you're lucky: there are lots of books and courses available and you have people like myself and others to help you. I had no one except Angie, and even though she was annoying me by demanding we go and have lunch, I was not going to let go of this opportunity to get into the property business.

This house was laid out to provide 5 bedrooms and near to the college where I worked, and so I thought it would be ideal for my students. It had heavily patterned, very dated Axminster carpets, the type which seem to last forever. I would have ripped them out, but for Angie's advice. I later discovered they were ideal for students, as when they were sick on them, it did not look so bad. On some walls was heavy red flock wallpaper very much like they used to put in Indian restaurants, which was beginning to peel off. The house had generally seen better days and needed a refurbishment.

The lunch with Angie must have been the best value for money meal I had ever purchased. She told me that students (we are talking about 1991) didn't care about carpet, wallpaper and things like that, as they would redecorate it themselves. How, I was to later find out! She also acted as my mentor and guided me through rudimentary letting and management processes, which I discovered were no big deal and largely common-sense.

How do you think I bought the property? Remember I

was 'just over broke', but I had a professional status. Ask yourself, what comes with this? Good credit! This is how I financed my first house. I applied for every credit card I could and built up a collection of about 20 of them. Then, I used the cash advances they offer to buy property.

I remember being ridiculed for this. I was told credit cards were expensive and were for paying for holidays, buying food and clothes etc, not for securing your financial future! However, I knew the truth. It is not what it costs, but what you make that is important. Don't worry about the price of the shovel when you're digging for gold. It's fair enough to be careful with what you spend, but don't let penny-pinching get in the way of making a deal. It is this outside-the-rational, almost reckless behaviour, which I later recognised as the hallmark of the entrepreneur. I have seen it time and time again and I admit I am tame in comparison. Unfortunately, my wife did not appreciate me buying property. She felt I was putting our financial future in jeopardy, and left me.

Despite borrowing most of the purchase price using 'expensive' credit cards, my first house still turned a profit of about £3k in its first year. This was about 25% of my take-home pay as a college lecturer, and it gave me enormous satisfaction and the impetus to buy more property.

That first property I purchased cost me £35k. Within 17 years it was valued on its income at £350k and had a gross rent of £36k. Deducting bills gave a net profit of about £30k – exactly what I had been earning three years earlier as a law lecturer when I took voluntary redundancy in 2004. In 17 years that one property replaced my income – awesome!

It is only on reflection I realised how easy it was to get into property and I wish I had started earlier and had done more. Initially, I was very timid and didn't take full advantage of the opportunities. I started my property journey late in life and far too slowly. This is a business which can take over 20 years to become successful!

I could have purchased and run a yacht on what I had missed out on if I had started 20 years earlier. Hardly a success story! I hope my story inspires you to do better than I did.

3. **Question:** Who was your first mentor?

   Answer: My first mentor, I suppose, was my college accommodation officer. I was a lecturer when I purchased my first HMO, and she helped me buy my first HMO and guided me through the letting and management process. I discovered it was no big deal and largely common-sense. But we (or should I say I) are scared of what we don't know. Now I help others to get over this with HMO Daddy's 'HMO Academy', where HMO newbies work in my business, which manages about 140 HMOs and nearly 1,000 tenants, and learn how to do it by working with the professionals.

For details of the 'HMO Academy' see my website: www.hmodaddy.com

4. **Question:** Jim, how did you get a law degree if you came from a children's home?

Answer: In my day it did not take any money to get a degree, as there were grants for education. Degree courses were free for the poor! Looking back, it was easy; all you needed was belief in yourself and the ability to study. I am surprised and puzzled why more people did not do what I did. The general perception at that time was getting a degree was only for the wealthy, privileged and bright. It wasn't even true then, which I think people have now begun to realise. A bit like how to get into property today except, perhaps, that to get into property you also need to be an enormous risk taker, who believes things will work out and a bit of a rule bender. Be warned, anal rule followers and perfectionists struggle at being an HMO landlord.

5. **Question:** Knowing what you know now, would you have still expanded your portfolio to the size it is?

Answer: I am not sure. I am a typical Libran, so I'm always weighing things up. A large portfolio brings benefits, but with an enormous number of problems. However, I would have regretted not 'playing the game to the fullest' if I had kept to a smaller number of properties. Being a certain scale allows the luxury of a staff to take on the tedious tasks of running properties. I find staffing issues frustrating, but certainly not boring. Some of the other issues of being a large employer are:

i. **Tall Poppy Syndrome**

Property is an area which local authorities like to take an interest in and some are clearly out to attack you. They see you as the enemy: a greedy landlord in competition with their grossly inefficient and highly-subsidised social housing. Councils get paid up to ten times what I get to house single people in very similar accommodation. More than one council official has seen it as their role to have a pop at me. Luckily, they were not very clever at it and got it wrong. I have even had the Council misapplying the law to try and get me. Truly appalling behaviour.

ii. **Litigation**

The larger you get, the more likely people are to sue

you. Research shows that you are more likely to get sued if someone dislikes you and the chances are multiplied if you have staff. However hard you try, there is always one member of staff who does not care a damn and upsets tenants. If they can, they will sue you, aided at no cost to themselves by 'no win, no fee solicitors'. Even more gallingly, mostly it's the result of their own incompetence, like tripping on stairs. Staff, especially the ones you have gone out of your way to help, often turn on you. Watch out for unfair dismissal claims, another appalling piece of legislation. Win or lose, the employer (you) will have to pay.

6. **Question:** I noticed you received a barrage of criticism after appearing on the TV. Why did you do it?

   Answer: I did not realise at the time that it would lead to so much criticism, but I was surprised just how many people could see through the distorted view of me the documentary presented.

   Although I am constantly criticised by those in authority and the chattering classes, I believe I do a very good job at what I do. Most of the accommodation I provide is warm, modern, clean, fully furnished and of a standard well above average for HMOs in terms of management, condition and fire safety. I accept they are not the Hilton, but far better than living on the streets. I also provide support for my tenants. I am proud to say I have never knowingly evicted a tenant who could not pay, only those who refuse to pay (although unfortunately there are an awful lot of those). The ones I cannot understand are those who refuse to claim Housing Benefit, which pays the rent for the low paid and unemployed. Some twisted logic applies with some of them and, when challenged, they sometimes reply they don't want charity, yet they happily claim unemployment pay and are prepared to sponge off me. Bizarre! I have lost tens of thousands of pounds a year by being soft on non-payers.

At the time, I agreed to appear on the programme, I felt that there were very few landlords prepared to put over the landlord's point of view, not realising just how the media twist and select what bits they report so as to often give a distorted view. They are rarely interested in portraying the reality or truth.

Even today I come across people who criticise me based on what they saw on TV. When I explain to them the position, and I invite them up to see the reality themselves, some decline saying they do not need to, as they know all about me from what they saw on TV!

Whether I would do it again, I am not sure.

7. **Question:** Jim, why do you write so much?

   Answer: To put it simply, I write because I like to. I find it therapeutic; it is a whim that I have the luxury to indulge. What motivates me to get up in the morning is doing something that interests me. I don't need the money and most of what I do has little or no return. Conversely, there is nothing else I do that can beat the return I get from creating an HMO, especially one with 10+ beds that could yield £40k annually once set up, if you ran it yourself.

8. **Question:** What made you buy so many properties?

   Answer: It was in 2004, 13 years after I started, when I had 38 properties (20 of them HMOs) that I decided that I would like to expand and have 100 HMOs. It seemed a good idea at the time. There are plenty of valid reasons to have more properties. The best is just owning a property and waiting for about 20 years for it to quadruple in price. This is to me the most compelling reason to own property. In the 13 years I had been operating, the first properties I acquired had seen awesome increases in value, and rents had also increased. Whether property will continue to increase in value outside the South East is unknown. In the last 12 years (i.e. since 2004) I have seen little increase in my property values. Outside the South East, most properties have not got back to their 2008 values.

Along with the benefit of investing in property, another motivation to expand was simply that I was getting tired of doing mindless repetitive tasks. I've never had a grand master plan – I bought more properties partly to pay for the staff I decided to employ. Property is a service industry. You, as a landlord, are providing a service to your tenants: fetching this, repairing that, cleaning, preparing, collecting rent and doing viewings – along with being to blame for everything! It was the fetching and carrying that got me down. My breaking point was taking a TV to a tenant at 9pm on a Friday, who complained that it did not have an aerial. At that time, I supplied TVs free of charge. The tenant had not asked for an aerial, and it would take me the best part of an hour to go and fetch one. Not unreasonably, I wanted to go home and eat. I had a full-time job at the time, and ran a business along with my property portfolio. I thought how nice it would be to employ staff to do all the fetching and carrying, never realising that I was going to unleash a monster of staffing issues. No one it seems, apart from me, will tell you the truth about staff (or much else about this business for that matter).

Getting back to that decision to employ staff, I felt I needed to have more properties to cover the cost of employing staff. Also, if I could manage 38 properties (20 of which were HMOs) by myself while I had a full-time job and ran a business, logic dictated I would need more properties to keep my staff occupied. I had not realised that staff do not behave or act the same way as I do. At that time, I had a full-time handyman and a part-time person who I kindly called a general manager. The latter would sort out bits and pieces when I was not available (which was most of the time during working hours). If I needed other people I would employ them, as and when, and it was a nightmare. You could never get them when you wanted them; the cost of employing them was all over the place and was sometimes extortionate.

To have full-time employees available seemed ideal. I remember counting the number of appointments I made with a plumber that he failed to attend, which was eight. Never a word of apology, nothing was his fault. Now I have two full-time plumbers working for me and it seems like luxury compared to those days – now I can pick up the phone and get a plumbing issue dealt with immediately and it is a luxury I savour. Yes, sad I know! But we all have our own idiosyncrasies! Previously I would spend over 30 minutes on the phone pleading to get a plumber who would agree to turn up in a day or two's time. I would arrange to meet them, but they would fail to turn up and so on. The wasted time was enormous. So that is why I went large. At the time, I thought scale allowed you to support a level of fixed overhead that yields massive convenience, but at a price that would crush a small operation.

9. **Question:** Do you make much money out of writing books and running courses?

Answer: Nothing I can think of compares to the long-term returns that can be made from property, especially HMOs. The hundreds of hours I spend running courses, writing articles and books such as this are unlikely to provide more than a miniscule return, if any. They take even more effort to sell! However, I enjoy the process even though I am not very good at it. My use of English and spelling is appalling, my proofreading skills are bad and I am a very slow writer and spend an enormous amount of time revising what I write. Writing, along with running courses and doing speaking engagements, makes but frugal returns, nowhere near the potential return from properties, but is less risky.

10. **Question:** What motivated you to go into property?

Answer: Let me take you back over forty years to 1971. Even though I was raised in a children's home, this is not a tale of rags to riches but missed opportunity, as I will explain as I go along. Let me ask you a question:

Have you ever wanted to do something,
yet fear held you back?

In those days, they kicked you out of the children's home at the age of 15, so I ended up drifting around and finally joined the merchant navy. I started off working on luxury passenger ships and quickly became the top silver service waiter on board, serving at the captain's table. I loved traveling the world, with free food and accommodation and, above all, the comradeship. The sheer decadence of it all was in total contrast to the austere children's homes of the 60s of my youth. I could eat as much as I wanted of the very best food while I travelled the world for free. By the time I was 20, I had been around the world. It was great; I was living the life! However, my Scottish Presbyterian past pulled me back. My upbringing insisted that life was not for enjoyment and I should get a proper job, which meant I should learn a trade or profession. So I needed to get a qualification. I therefore saved up, while working in the navy, to pay my way through college.

I rented a bedsit in Clapham, South London, while studying for my A levels to achieve my goal of going to university.

The landlord Mr. Schult thought I was great, as I was motivated to get qualifications, while his teenage children had no aspirations whatsoever. We got talking and he told me he bought his first property for £3k seven years previously in 1964, which was now worth £20k. The house had risen 667%, or £17k, in value in just seven years! In 1971, £17k was an awesome sum of money – a good wage being £1k a year. To put it into today's money, the property had gone up by about £100k per year. I remember thinking this was the business to be in. Should I give up on education and instead purchase a house to let as bedsits? Despite the enormous opportunity dangling before me, my ignorance and fear of the unknown held me back. I don't know, but maybe he would have helped me if I had bothered to ask. He may even have managed the property and I could have returned to my real love, the merchant navy. I poignantly regret that I did not follow this up and, instead got a degree and became a college lecturer. I think it was this bedsit in Clapham which gave me the idea to become a property investor. Unfortunately, it took me until 1991 to take action and get into property. Imagine what I could have achieved with a 20-year head start! If you share my entrepreneurial urges, join us at www.hmodaddy.com to find out how we can help you make your ambitions a reality.

11. **Question:** Why is it that you are so different from other speakers I have heard? You tell it as it is.

   Answer: Maybe it is because I have the luxury of having an opinion without responsibility. Most of those working and who are knowledgeable of the housing field have clients, customers' expectations or businesses to support.

A business provider is hardly likely to say you do not need their services unless they are using psychologically manipulative sales games. They will always say that you need more of their services, not less. If you employed every specialist and consultant that considered themselves essential you would consign yourself to financial oblivion.

I talk and teach because I want to. I enjoy it; it is a bit of a paid hobby. I do not have to worry about making a profit, yet perversely I do rather well out of it. Then again, there may be another reason: perhaps I am being stupid. I appreciate that my forthright views put a lot of people off joining my courses and upsets those in authority. They find criticism, especially when true, hard to take.

12. **Question:** My name is Fred, I am 26 and a teacher I have come to realize that if I want to get ahead in life I have to act now. I have been doing some research in property and how to start up and have become very interested in how you managed to become such a success from a small start-up. It's amazing!

You have become an inspiration to me and I would like to know what makes you happiest in your life and what enables you to have a balanced life.

Are there any skills which you think are the most

important to learn to help get started in this area of the market?

Who was your inspiration in life and business?

If you could go back in time would there be anything you would do differently?

Answer: Thank you for the compliments. However, if you are looking to me as an example of a person to follow, you will be disappointed. My why and life balance is irrelevant. It is yours that matters. I can show you how to find, run and finance HMOs, and almost uniquely, without having any money yourself. But only if you are sufficiently motivated and have the ability to take risks, amongst other traits.

I would love to help you, please contact me at: jim@hmodaddy.com

13. **Question:** Why is it that you seem so relaxed about doing deals?

    Answer: Initially, I was not relaxed doing deals – I was scared and uncertain. When I lost a deal (even though it cost me money in legal and valuation fees), I would heave a sigh of relief. It is because I have done so many that I am now so relaxed, which is dangerous as I could come unstuck. I need to constantly remind myself you are only one deal away from financial ruin.

During my time, I have acquired what many thought were bad deals. Now their sniggers are silent and forgotten as I have laughed all the way to the bank. Property has been very kind to me and all my deals have worked out. I think the only thing you can do wrong with property is to not buy it and if you have bought then to sell it! I am not the calm, confident, relaxed person most people think I am and I get very stressed or frustrated with certain things. I wish I could be like the spy in the film 'Bridge of Spies' who, when caught and facing execution, was asked by his lawyer why he did not seem concerned. The Russian spy replied, 'Would it help?'

CHAPTER 2
HOW TO GET STARTED

*These are the questions I like, as I feel deeply privileged
to help those who are brave enough to dare to start.
It takes enormous guts!*

14. **Question:** I want to get into the property business and I
    am told HMOs are the thing to do, but I do not have very
    much money or idea of how to do it. Can you advise me
    on what I need to do to get started?

    Answer: The property business is over 90% dependent
    on your self-belief and ability to take risks followed by
    tenacity and consistency, amongst others. There is no
    guarantee that some of the strategies used in the
    property business will work. Nor will there ever be – it

is more an act of faith. Further, what worked previously may not work today, just as what works today may not work tomorrow. Strategies often have a limited life span: for example, Same-Day Re-Mortgaging, Sale and Rent Back, etc.

Money distorts peoples' objectives, and only plays a very small part in the property business. Worse, it can even get in the way and its lack is often used as an excuse for inactivity. Some knowledge is essential (and there are plenty of books and courses around today which can show you how to do it), but the rest is just confidence, attitude and motivation. I am not saying you do not need any money, but its significance is over-estimated. Strategies such as Rent to Rent, Rent to Buy, Delayed Completions, Vendor Finance and Adverse Possession can, with lots of luck, be done with very little or no money.

15. **Question:** I just keep hitting problems with my attempts at starting to build my HMO portfolio. Have you any tips on what to do?

   Answer: Emotional problems like stress are fundamentally down to how you handle them. These problems are only a problem if you let them get to you. As a businessperson you have to learn that you do not have problems, only opportunities – with a 'bring it on' attitude, we can deal with anything. Be a problem-solving machine. Believe that opportunities are all around you and you will find them, but you need to be clear what it is that you want.

16. **Question:** Would you say I should start off in HMOs or start with professional renting first and then go into HMOs?

    Answer: I am not sure what you mean by 'professional renting'. If you mean single-lets, then it is up to you. The yields from single lets, even in my area near Birmingham, result in very little profit so you will be relying on capital appreciation. I prefer HMOs as they give a good income that you need to live on today. Relying on capital appreciation is volunteering to become a hostage of economics and/or circumstances beyond your control. Most people lack the patience to win at this long-term game and they give up at the first sign of a small capital profit. I started with HMOs and if I was to start again it would be HMOs – the bigger the better!

17. **Question:** what is the main attribute you need to become an HMO landlord?

    Answer: Despite what you'd think, factors like having financing, a good credit record, knowledge of the business, and a power team are all pretty well insignificant. They help, but the essential attribute is your mindset. The ability to accept risk is critical. You must have the attitude that "it will all work out in the end". There are no guarantees in property and there never were. Sensible souls who love to ask 'what if ...', 'what about ...' are unlikely to become HMO landlords as the road to becoming an HMO landlord is mired in uncertainty and risk!

I sometimes struggle to answer questions about demand for HMO rooms, property suitability, tenant type, property condition, attitude of the council, regulations, legality, ability to get finance and lots more. All I can say with certainty is: this is how I do it and it clearly works for me. However, I can't make that leap of faith for you and it's something you have to learn to be comfortable with.

The more I look into this business the more I believe it is more an act of faith and luck!

18. **Question:** How much work is involved in buying and setting up an HMO?

Answer: I have never analysed the time it takes me to find and set up an HMO, but a lot has to do with its location and size. Distant properties eat up more travelling time and bigger HMOs require longer building works. I estimate my minimum time input is two to three weeks' work to find and set up an HMO. However, this time will be spread well over a year from finding, to refurbishing to letting. Most purchases take over a month and the conversion work can take over six months. It can be over two years before I see a return. And this, after 25 years of experience, systems and contacts!

TIMELINE TO CREATE AN HMO		
ACTION	**TIME**	**WORK**
To find a property	Variable	4 – 40 hours
Purchase	Well over a month	2 – 4 hours
Supervising building work	Well over six months	12 – 52 hours
Applying for a re-mortgage	Well over three months	4 – 20 hours
TOTALS	**At least 10 months**	**22 – 116 hours**

Letting to unemployed tenants means further months of delay as the rent is usually paid four weeks in arrears and it can take up to eight weeks for the Housing Benefit claim to be processed.

19. **Question:** I have little money, so is there much point in me enrolling on your HMO Mastery?

Answer: The benefit of being an HMO Mastery mentee is access to me and my team – we have well over 30 years experience between us! Add to this the power of my whole team and the potential to get you commercial financing.

If you have little money, seek out a suitable property where the owner is prepared to do a delayed completion and give you immediate occupancy for little or no rent and deposit. Then you can convert the property into an HMO, and once the property is fully let, you can apply for commercial mortgage to fund the purchase and the return of any money spent. In other words, 'property for nothing, money for free', using the bank's money! On HMO Mastery, we can give you the help, skills and contacts so you can do this. Once you grasp this concept, you will see what an awesome opportunity HMO Mastery is. Unlike flipping, you also get paid forever, providing you manage your HMO well.

For details of my HMO Mastery, please see my website: www.hmodaddy.com

20. **Question:** I would like to be a large HMO landlord like you. How do I go about it?

Answer: My simple answer is – don't! Keep to a small portfolio.

There is an old Chinese proverb which says, 'be careful what you wish for'. The same goes with property. There is a reason why most HMO landlords only have 5 to 20 HMOs. I will explain why!

It is to do with the management of HMOs. Most HMO landlords find they can comfortably manage up to 20 HMOs themselves, or up to 10 HMOs if they have a full-time job. There is no law regarding this number of properties, it is the product of my observation over many years. I used to manage over 20 HMOs along with about 18 single-lets while working full time and running a business, although I accept I may be an exception.

The problem – and this is one of the unspoken taboos in our society – is staff! Once you get above a certain size, you have to employ staff. Irrespective of whether they are self-employed, agents or employees, the outcome is no different. I have tried them all, and with all, you have a management issue. Everyone who has been an employee thinks it is easy to manage staff, while employers know the truth! Ignore anyone who tries to give you advice if they aren't an employer; my experience is that it is a lot easier to manage your HMOs yourself than try and manage staff to do it for you. For more on employing staff, get my manual 'Employing an HMO manager' only available from www.hmodaddy.com

I feel that many HMO landlords (also single-let landlords) create a lot of extra work for themselves by getting others to manage their properties for them instead of doing it themselves. It is far easier to manage properties yourself, but you need to learn to multi-task, blocking jobs and evaluate what you do. Many people do not appreciate how easy it is to manage your own property and have self-limiting beliefs about their capabilities and an exaggerated perception about the problems they may encounter. This assumes that your properties are local so that you can self manage them. If your HMOs are over 30 minutes from where you live you will struggle to self manage them and need to employ someone to look after them.

On average, five HMOs kept for twenty years will make you a very comfortable living, so why bother with anything more?

21. **Question:** What is the best course to do if I want to be an HMO landlord?

   Answer: This is a common question I am asked and I find it frustrating because it shows a lack of understanding of the business.

   Firstly, some courses may give you an understanding of a particular aspect of HMO management, but do you seriously believe that a one-day event or a one day a month course over a year is going to make you competent, much less an expert, in anything? Most of the so-called gurus in this industry invest regularly in their personal development and I have bumped into them on courses.

I doubt any single course is sufficient and you can never go on too many. For example, Rent-to-Rent hardly existed ten years ago and now those who succeed adapt to a changing market by regular contact with those who are doing it. If you are serious, you need to do the same – such company can give you the edge.

Try and avoid inventing the wheel over and over again and take advantage of the advice that is out there. One deal can make you tens of thousands of pounds, against which the cost of a book, course or mentorship pales in significance.

Secondly, and probably more importantly, if you need a course rather than want or wouldn't mind doing a course, then you are probably starting from the wrong place. Many of the high-flyers in this industry never did any courses before starting, they just did it. I know this goes against the grain and I may be talking myself out of business, but as people tell me, I say it as it is. There is no teacher better than experience. So the question should be: why are you not doing it already? The reality for most of us is that we lack confidence, belief or motivation. We invent reasons or barriers for not doing something, which when you have done it, you wonder why you did not do it a long time ago. Often, when you have done it you appear to others as arrogant for forgetting the barriers you overcame, as they seem silly in retrospect or you realise they were not barriers at all. Now that I am doing more mentoring, people are coming to me with issues that could have derailed them without my reassurance. To give three recent examples:

i. 'Rent-to-rent is illegal' – a council tax official.

ii. 'You cannot multi-let without planning permission' – a planning officer.

iii. 'You cannot get mortgages on HMOs' – a mortgage broker.

None of the above are true – as I reassured my mentees. Officials who 'should know better' often don't, or worse often lie!

22. **Question:** If you were just starting out, only had £35k to your name, in this current market with the new laws, what would your plan be and how would you grow your portfolio?

Answer: I would not start from your point, though having £35k is a good start. If you have saved £35k, then this shows enormous ability to control your finances. Before I started, assuming I was in full-time regular employment I would do four things:

First: read up on the subject.

Second: Attend value-for-money property training program which gives you ongoing support from those who are currently active in property and preferably offer on the job training i.e. you can work in a HMO business.

Third: Appreciate you will be putting yourself under enormous emotional and mental strain. Read and if you can attend personal development courses which can support you In this area.

Finally: Obtain as much credit as possible. You need to use other people's money to get the best from property. Borrow money at below 10% per annum and make more than 10% on your HMOs. You make money on the margin. You will need a big margin as the lender will often want capital repayments. Currently I am borrowing at 5%, but this effectively increases to about 9% with capital repayments over 15 to 20 years. Note that capital repayments are not allowable for tax, so it comes out of taxed income.

The ways a working person with a good credit rating can increase their credit is by obtaining:

a) Credit cards – every card will give you £500 - £10,000 of credit.

b) Bank overdrafts – usually £1k to £5k.

c) Personal loans – £10k - £25k.

If you do it right (learn how to do it correctly before you start), you should build yourself at least an additional £200k of available credit. Property is very cash hungry and you need to be very careful with your budgeting so you do not run out of money. Above all, do not delay in starting – spend weeks not months on the above.

23. **Question:** I am told I should get a mentor to help me in my property journey, what do you think?

Answer: Originally, I thought I did it all by myself. On reflection, though I have never had what I would call a property mentor, I have relied at times on people for advice (not always good!). I would not have achieved what I did without help. I am sure I would have achieved more, faster, with a good mentor. When I started the accommodation officer at my college guided me through what to do, but later took advantage by offloading her undesirable tenants onto me.

The dilemma is not whether to have a mentor, but how to find a good mentor. The critical test is: 'Is this person helping me to go forward'. If not, why? In the end, you have to make your own decisions.

From observation, I have noted that most high-flyers admit to having a mentor, so perhaps you and I should get one!

24. **Question:** However hard I try I don't seem to get anywhere in my search for properties. What am I doing wrong?

Answer: This business can suck. In my experience it does not follow the normal rules of business which say the harder you work the more successful you are. Obviously, if you do nothing then you get nothing. Property appears to reward those who are relaxed, but can react lightning-quick when an opportunity arises. Often it is difficult to spot a deal and most would not spot one if it hit them. I have found that trying does not make that much difference, a marginal one at best, and may be a distraction. You often get the same results with patience and being prepared. You will occasionally stumble across opportunities, but you only have seconds to react. I shudder to think just how many opportunities I have lost, not to mention the revenue!

It is the ability to assess a deal quickly and have the guts to take it that is the hallmark of the successful investor. You only need a few property deals to set yourself up for life, especially if you hold instead of flipping. The problem with flipping is you are only as rich as the next deal – it is just a job, though at times a very lucrative one. With holding, you buy once and are paid twice; first in rental income, which can be very high if you multi-let the property, and second by capital appreciation. You can draw this out by re-mortgaging and it is tax-free.

I suggest you join a property group and discuss the opportunities you have seen, learn to evaluate them, and maybe consider looking at other areas.

CHAPTER 3
TENANT ISSUES

Tenants are the most important aspect of the whole business and it is crucial we focus on this issue.

25. **Question:** Do you charge deposits?

Answer: No, I refused to participate on principle with a badly-drafted, unfair scheme. Instead I now charge an administration fee which I keep. There is no extra work to do when taking an administration fee compared to taking a deposit which involves a lot of tedious meticulous administration and you do not give the administration fee back when the tenant leaves. You also avoid the draconian penalties you can incur if you get any detail of the deposit scheme wrong as you can have a penalty of having to return the deposit plus up to three times the deposit. I do not see the advantage of taking a deposit, as I don't think it makes any difference to the behaviour of most of my tenants. Most just refuse to pay the last month's rent before they leave.

NB: It is proposed the law on taking administration fees and other charges is going to change. Until the detail is given I cannot comment, but I suspect it can easily be got around by, for example, charging a higher rent for the first month.

26. **Question:** I take two months' rent in advance to cover the first and last month's rent and do not take a deposit. I have heard you say that this is still a deposit?

Answer: Anything paid in advance above the normal rent period is a deposit if you return it at the end of the tenancy. It doesn't matter what you call it, it is still a DEPOSIT! Failure to protect a deposit means that tenant can sue you for the deposit, plus 3 times the deposit, plus possible extra problems with evicting your tenants.

If you want to take two months' rent, then legally you can do this but the next rent due date has to be two months later and so on. Be very careful with deposits, as solicitors have now caught on to suing landlords who have not followed the rules and are helping tenants sue for the return of their deposit plus three times the deposit.

27. **Question:** Do you get your tenant to agree/sign an inventory to confirm the condition of the room when they move in? What do you include in it?

Answer: I have a standard agreement for all my tenants – understand that I let to professionals, workers, students and the unemployed. I gave up with inventories a long ago, as it is of little use with the unemployed and some workers. If tenants damage or steal, there is nothing you can do about it. The police will not usually take any interest, dismissing it as a civil matter. Worse, they might take hours of your time in giving a statement, but if they catch the thief they will do very little. They have even let my tenants keep the stuff they stole. The reality is that theft by a tenant is not often treated as a crime in this country.

In the 25 years I have been a landlord, I have never had a tenant worth suing who caused loss or damage to property that I felt justified in pursuing, but I am very relaxed and allow a lot for wear and tear. The only case I can recollect is a student who, between check-out and my giving him his deposit back, managed to steal a desk chair which only cost £29 new, so its second-hand value was negligible.

Is the time in doing an inventory worth the effort? With me, the answer is no. In my landlord forms and letters (manual/USB only available from www.hmodaddy.com), I have a brief list of what is included and we photograph the room and tenant. That is all we do.

28. **Question:** Do you have a check-out process for when your tenants leave?

Answer: Most of my tenants abandon, or say they have left after they have left. It is very rare for a tenant to give notice and ask to be checked out. Unfortunately, this is the reality of what some landlords face. When I used to take deposits back in 2005, if a tenant called me to ask for his deposit back and to arrange a check-out, it was so unusual I often gave them their deposit back without even checking. This type of tenant was likely to do things in the right way and so there were rarely any problems. Check-outs and inventories only apply if you let to professionals, of which I have very few, and they are never a problem. Yes, in say one in fifty cases there will be a problem, but is the time spent on the other forty-nine worth it? I suspect check-ins and check-outs are an invention of letting agents as they can charge for doing it, but in my experience it is not a worthwhile process.

29. **Question:** Jim, you can't still be a hands-on landlord with the number of tenants you have?

Answer: Take a look in the boot of a landlord's car and you will find out just how hands-on or not they are! In mine, you will find tenancy paperwork and agreements, tools, a plunger, light bulbs, extension leads, electric heaters (for supplying to tenants when the central heating breaks down), lock barrels, dustpan and brush, mop and bucket, etc.

30. **Question:** I find the attitude of some of my tenants awful. How did you learn to cope with them?

Answer: Probably, my early experience in the merchant navy helped – passengers could be viewed as a pain or who you are paid to serve. This helped me a lot when dealing with tenants. My upbringing in a children's home and my early years as a lecturer had acclimatised me to being treated with contempt and ridicule, something you need to get used to as a landlord. To be fair, over 99% of my tenants are wonderful and only very few are a pain. I find it helps that I take the view that a bad tenant is partly my fault, as you have the discretion whether or not to take them. If you get a bad one, learn from your mistakes and move on.

31. **Question:** How, do you manage to stop tenants breaking into secured boiler cupboard to turn up the heating controls?

Answer: This is a problem we have all the time, usually with LHA tenants. Some go further and smash up the boiler, usually out of frustration, because it has broken down. In one year, we replaced just under 10% of our boilers because the tenants had deliberately attacked them or messed with them, causing them to over-pressure and necessitating their replacement. We now fit pressure limiters to all boilers, which prevents this.

However, the answer is not to deny them central heating just because a small minority abuse it. It is an unfortunate overhead that you will simply have to get used to.

I envy many of my LHA tenants, as they seem immune to the law. If you report the damage to the police, they will probably say it is a civil matter. If you persist, they will take a statement, which will take hours, and then say that there is no proof as the tenant has denied doing it! Even if it could be proved, it is very unlikely to result in court action. Even then, the tenant will probably get a small fine, if that!

32. **Question:** Jim, just wonder whether you could share your experience and advise me on my case. I am currently doing an eviction. Happily, the tenant didn't have any rent arrears, but just refused to move out (we need to convert the house into two flats). I applied for "Accelerated process section 21A" and received the possession order (surprisingly no hearing!) and then applied for a Bailiff's Order. The Bailiff's Order is for 22nd January to evict them. I am not sure whether the bailiff will be able to evict them on the day as the tenant is a single mum and has two children. She wasn't single when her husband approached us initially and said only he and his wife will move into the house, but now she has two little children, recently divorced her husband,

and her husband has moved out from the house. So she is now claiming that she is a single mum with two children. I have been to see the court manager yesterday and applied for extra bailiffs. Not sure whether they will give us more (or police) on the day to help evict her. I think this is going to be a difficult one.

Just wonder whether you had any cases in the past where the bailiff came but still couldn't evict the tenant?

Answer: No, never. The bailiffs have always evicted, and even in one case dragged the tenant out. Most of the time the tenants have left before the bailiffs called. However, I am the wrong person to ask about this as I only evict for cause, i.e. rent arrears or bad behaviour. I don't think it is right to evict without good cause. I have never evicted a tenant who is behaving and paying. I have properties which I have wanted to convert, but I have always waited until the tenants have left under their own freewill. I am sure there are plenty of other deals you can do in the meantime. I believe it is important for landlords to do the best for their tenants, so have you considered finding your tenant alternative accommodation? As she has children, she is eligible to be re-housed by the council when you evict her. When I evict, I liaise with the council and come to a consensual agreement giving the council time to re-house so as to avoid the need to apply for bailiffs. Thankfully, all my tenants consider being housed by the council a good option. I would strongly urge you to do this, talk to your council and call off the bailiffs. Consider the impact your actions will have on the young children, the stress on the single mother, never mind the bad publicity your action will have on the perception of landlords.

Yes, you will lose your bailiff fee of £110 and you will need to re-apply should the tenants not leave, but I feel this is the right thing to do. I am surprised the council have not been in touch and asked you to do this (they usually do).

33. **Question:** I think I do a good job for my tenants yet I still get complaints. Do you have this problem Jim?

    Answer: Yes, and it is not only the tenants you will have problems with as an HMO landlord, but also the anti-landlord attitudes by many in the council and neighbours. Do not expect those from your council to approve or help you, they are often very anti-HMO. I have come to accept that in our society those who do good are often ridiculed, yet crooks, gangsters, spongers and hedonists are rarely criticised, if not revered. That private landlords (especially HMO landlords) provide accommodation at a fraction of the cost, and with greater tenant satisfaction, than the highly-subsidised social sector is one of the many unreported unfairnesses of modern life.

34. **Question:** I have a room left in very poor condition and was going to renovate it. A builder approached me saying he would like the room as it was, as he could do it up himself, and was more interested in getting a lower rent and not paying a deposit. The builder then went to the council complaining about how bad the room was. I am now having a lot of grief from the council and they are not interested in what I and the tenant agreed. The builder is now refusing to pay rent due to the condition of the room. What should I do?

Answer: Do the works and then evict for non-payment of rent. If you do it the other way around, then the tenant could defend the action and counterclaim for disrepair. Once the work is done, this excuse is less likely to work. I suspect the tenant will still not pay and so you will have good grounds for evicting them for nonpayment of rent.

Though you had made a perfectly reasonable agreement, the law is not on your side. The room has to be in a lettable state and you cannot let a room which is not in good condition. I suspect the builder knew this and has done the same thing before!

35. **Question:** I have a tenant who alleges they have tripped on some frayed carpet on my stairs and injured

themselves. I do not believe that he tripped or was injured. I received a letter from one of those 'no win, no fee' solicitors demanding that I supply a long list of information or the name of my insurer, which I ignored and heard nothing for months. I have now received a further demand and they want me to pay them £800 or they will take me to court. Can they do this?

Answer: I am not a solicitor and you should obtain legal advice. All I can do is tell you my experience.

The system is that with a personal injury claim, all the solicitor has to do is assert a claim. I have had claims which are nothing more than three lines long. If you are insured, as you ought to be, your insurers will deal with the claim. Otherwise, you as the defendant will have to. If you deal with the claim, then you are required by law to disclose certain information. You have to, in effect, disprove the claim or assist the claimant's solicitor, who is entitled to make an application to court for disclosure regardless of the merits of the claim and its costs. I have seen some in excess of £1,200 – not bad for a few hours' work! I feel these solicitors are often quick in making an application to the court, giving very little warning of their intentions. This enables them to claim fees for nothing more than making an application for disclosure, as the claim itself does not have to proceed.

36. **Question**: I went on a one-day course yesterday and they made a big song and dance about detailed inventories, photos and videos. I can see the relevance in a standard BTL, but in an HMO? The tenant is responsible for the contents and condition of their room. Fine. But what about the communal areas and kitchen, etc.? If the TV goes missing or the fridge loses a shelf what happens? How can you withhold part of the deposit for wear and tear in a bathroom when all the tenants are probably liable? I know you avoid deposits, but you must still face this challenge.

I've thought about not taking a deposit and charging a non-refundable administration fee instead like you, but holding a deposit has a way of making a tenant feel a little more responsible towards the property.

Grateful for any HMO Daddy pragmatic tips.

Answer: Glad you did the course and not me! It just reinforces my view of some sectors of the market that spend too much time flogging their useless services instead of giving landlords good advice. Did you pay for this course?

Inventories only work for lets to quality students and the professional end of the market, not for working or unemployed tenants. They are only of use against those who you can sue or have guarantors with assets.

Further, the courts and the mediation services will usually only award second-hand value of goods lost or damaged, and you must produce substantial evidence to prove your case. 90% of my tenants don't have the assets to make it worthwhile suing them and the time spent on compliance would outweigh the benefit. Doing an inventory incurs a cost so that I could sue 1 in 100 and get what? The depreciated value of a carpet.

The only people you'll find trying to persuade you to use these services are selling them. Compare the compliance cost with the return and I suggest you will be grossly out of pocket. Talk to those who walk the walk, not the parasites who are great at selling but little else (other than trying to feed off landlords!).

37. **Question:** I received a letter out of the blue from a solicitor saying one of my tenants injured themselves in my property, which I referred to my insurers who settled. I am sure the tenant is just making up the claim. Is there anything I can do about it?

    Answer: I do not think so. There does not appear to be any comeback on the tenant or solicitor who brings these clearly fatuous actions. Nor is there any checking of the validity of the tenant's claim by the solicitor. To give an example I had: one of my tenants alleged that he twisted his ankle due to a stair handrail breaking, a good month after he went to hospital! I congratulated my tenant on his foresight in going to hospital a month *before* his accident and told them I would be defending the claim. I heard nothing more on this matter.

This sorry state of affairs continues because landlords refer such claims to their insurers, who settle the claim at the least cost by giving the claimant's solicitor a few thousand pounds to go away. A serious investigation would be much more expensive, so anything less than £5k is a reasonable result for the insurers.

However, by always settling, they are just encouraging further dubious claims. The insurers appear to be so terrified by the enormity of the awards that are given for personal injury claims that they would prefer to settle quietly. I doubt this is in the best interest of the genuine claimant, but it gives the solicitor a quick return and is a lower cost settlement for insurers. They worry that if the case went to court, the tenant could allege that they were crippled for life, were unable to work and claim millions of pounds in compensation. So the insurer is happy to pay a few thousand pounds for this risk to go away. The fraudulent and dubious claim is just a price of doing business for them and anyway, they can always pass the cost onto us by increased premiums!

38. **Question:** I have a tenant who made numerous threats to sue me, but thankfully is leaving after we agreed to pay her some rent back. How do I stop her coming back for more (which I strongly suspect she will try and do)?

   Answer: I am not a lawyer so you should seek your own legal advice. As I understand it there is no *certain* way you can stop a tenant coming back for more, but you are able to considerably reduce this likelihood by ensuring that she signs that payment is in 'full and final settlement'. A copy of the form I use, in a downloadable format (along with nearly 100 other forms I use), can be obtained on my website: www.hmodaddy.com.

   Once signed, it would be very difficult for your tenant to go back on the agreement. If you wanted more certainty, along with greater expense, have the tenant be advised by an independent solicitor. But this could backfire as the solicitor is duty bound to give the best advice, which will probably mean asking you for more money.

39. **Question:** I thought I was doing a favour for a new tenant. The ex-tenant left a load of stuff behind and, rather than throw it away, I told the new tenant to help himself as he was having a hard time and had little money. It turns out there was a toaster amongst the stuff, and my new tenant said the toaster blew up giving him an electric shock and distressing his little boy who

was visiting. The tenant has now turned from being very grateful to demanding compensation, otherwise he is going to get his solicitor to sue me. What do I do?

Answer: I am not a lawyer and unable to give legal advice. I can only tell you what I would do. You may be deep in the brown stuff and it only goes to prove my maxim that, 'no good deed an HMO landlord does, goes unpunished'. The issue, as I see it is: did you supply the electrical equipment or give it to the tenant? Either way you owe a duty of care, but much less if you gave it rather than supplied it. I also find the story of the toaster blowing up and giving an electric shock at the same time implausible unless he had stuck a knife or similar into it.

I would be very polite and say to the tenant that it is not working out and offer him his money back in 'full and final settlement' (even if he paid nothing) if he will leave. Such tenants are often looking for something for nothing and it could be a quick way of resolving the situation. A bad tenant only becomes worse (another of my maxims!) and I assure you that a tenant who wants to sue a landlord for giving him a hand-out will not be a good tenant.

Ensure the tenant signs a form that payment is in 'full and final settlement of all liabilities' (for a copy, see 'Forms and Letters for HMO landlords', only available at www.hmodaddy.com) and keep your fingers crossed.

40. **Question:** A tenant I suspect broke his own front door because he lost his keys, then claimed I was responsible for its repair. When I refused, he went to the council who said I was responsible and stated that this included windows even if broken by the tenant. The council officer also said that if I could prove it was caused by the tenant, I could sue the tenant. There is no point in suing the tenant, as he is unemployed. Is the council official correct in saying I must repair the damage caused by the tenant?

Answer: Yes, I am afraid so. You, the landlord, are responsible for the exterior structure of the building, however the damage is caused. I have had a tenant steal the lead off the roof, yet I am responsible for repairing it! The only thing you can do is evict the tenant (following a long and expensive process). As you say, there is no point in suing them.

I used to get a lot of problems with tenants breaking in because they had lost their keys. Sometimes they alleged that they had been broken into, while others just admitted it. This is why I offer a free 24/7 service to the tenants to let them in and replace their keys. It is now very rare a tenant breaks in, as they now just call us out.

CHAPTER 4
LETTING TO THE UNEMPLOYED AND HOMELESS

Letting to this sector is the most difficult, and sensible landlords avoid it when they can.

41. **Question:** Do you get any problems housing the homeless?

Answer: Yes, there is a minority of homeless people I have housed who have returned my help by not only failing to claim Housing Benefit, but also trashing the property. Often, far worse, some engage in drug taking and dealing (and other criminality), upset my other good tenants who have left and been a nuisance to neighbours. I am now very careful in selecting amongst those who are homeless who I will house.

42. **Question:** Jim, why do you house homeless people?

Answer: Because I get great pleasure in being able to help others and I know what it is like to be homeless. I was homeless myself after leaving care when I was fifteen (see question 10 and 44). I feel very privileged to be able to help house those who are homeless. I would like to say that I have never refused to house a genuinely homeless person who was capable of behaving in a tenant-like manner, just because they do not have any money to pay the rent. However, I will not house those who I feel will abuse their accommodation and it is very difficult to distinguish between the two.

I am not being as generous as I first appear with this, as we have a wonderful system in the UK where the state will pay if anyone cannot afford their rent. It was called Housing Benefit, now Universal Credit. Most products and services can only be transacted with consumers with money or access to credit. However, with housing, you can do business with anyone. This is irrespective of their ability to pay, provided their Housing Benefit entitlement covers the amount of rent you charge and they will actually claim it.

43. **Question:** Do you have many unemployed tenants?

Answer: My long-term average of the number of unemployed tenants that I housed up until 2008 was

6%. It currently stands at less than 20% and is reducing. During the recession, I had almost 60% unemployed tenants, the reason being that for almost four years after 2008 I had very, very few working tenants approach me for accommodation. We now accept fewer unemployed tenants and so avoid many problems.

44. **Question:** Jim, you say you will house homeless people, is this true?

Answer: Yes, I will house homeless people in some of my properties providing I am sure they will behave, pay the rent and treat my property with respect. One of the privileges of providing housing is the ability to help people who have had problems. I have a policy of helping others if I can, even if they do not have any money to pay me when they move in. However, due to many bad experiences, I am now very careful when housing homeless people and I reject over 90%. I regret that some of them might have been genuinely homeless, would have behaved, paid the rent, and have been capable of sustaining a tenancy unsupported.

I don't feel good about refusing to house these individuals, as I have been homeless myself. I was brought up in a children's home and in my day the state would kick you out at the age of 15, so I well appreciate the impact of not having a home. It is devastating to your psychological and physical well-being. Richard Gere's crusading film 'Time Out of Mind' about the plight of the homeless took me back to what I suffered all those years ago. At the time, I thought I was being a wimp. I told myself, 'Why should I worry? Toughen up, not having a home is not that bad!' Most of the adults I came into contact with had endured the hardship and devastation of war, compared to which being homeless was considered a trifle. Join the army if you needed somewhere to live, serve your country and become a man! This was the reaction in my day, so I just supressed my feelings.

Contemporary homeless people I have housed have a very different attitude. Good job I don't do it for the gratitude, because I do not get any! Too many of the homeless have turned out to be the tenants from hell, being verbally abusive and both I and my staff have felt at risk of physical assault. They take little responsibility for themselves, sometimes even failing to claim Housing Benefit. Those that do claim Housing Benefit can refuse to pay their Housing Benefit to their landlord and the system allows them to do this. Unbelievably, it is not a crime for the tenants to claim Housing Benefit and keep it. The tenants do not even have to repay the benefit they receive that they have kept and not paid to the landlord. Conversely, if the landlord kept benefit they were not entitled to, they could be prosecuted. Further, it takes two or three times longer to let to a homeless tenant, due to applying for Housing Benefit. Yet more time is required administrating the tenancy due to the concomitant bureaucracy, for which there is no financial compensation.

Worse, the homeless are also far more likely to be unsatisfactory tenants, damage the property and cause problems for my other tenants and neighbours. 99% of our problem tenants are also unemployed. To top off everything, the council (whom you are saving enormous amounts of money by housing the homeless and other vulnerable tenants for a fraction of the cost of the social sector) will often attack landlords and needlessly insist on adaptations to the property for little or no benefit to either tenant or landlord.

45. **Question:** I am told I am better off housing the unemployed as their rent is guaranteed. Is this true?

Answer: We have a wonderful system in the UK where, if anyone cannot afford their rent, the state will pay. It was called Housing Benefit, but is now part of the "Universal Credit". Thanks to this, with housing you can do business with anyone, unlike most products and services, where you can only do business if the buyer can afford to pay or get credit to pay. There are, however, at least four problems with taking Housing Benefit tenants.

First, from my experience, most of those who apply for housing with me and cannot afford to pay do not treat their housing with any respect and often badly abuse it. People clearly don't value what they don't pay for. Second, the system relies on the tenant claiming Housing Benefit and too many will claim to be far too busy and not co-operate! Unless the tenants fully co-operate, the landlord does not get paid. Third, the system is usually very slow and overcomplicated. It is full of traps for those who do not understand the system and is often badly administered to the disadvantage of the landlord. When taking housing benefit tenants, there is little emphasis on ensuring the landlord is paid correctly or at all. Unless you know your way around the system very well, you risk underpayment or non-payment. The system is obsessed with clawing back payments from the landlord under the guise of protecting the public purse, often without proper investigation. Finally, there are criminal sanctions if you get aspects of the claim wrong or fail to disclose certain information, such as that you are receiving rent and the tenant has left, even if you may not have known they have left!

It takes us two or three times longer to let to an unemployed tenant than a working tenant due to the extra time it takes to help them make a Housing Benefit application. However, if you do not help them make a claim, they are very unlikely to successfully do it themselves. You may also need to spend a lot of extra time in administrating the claim, for which you will not be paid.

Worse, lots of unemployed people I have housed have trashed the property, taken or dealt drugs, and committed other crimes. They have upset my other good tenants (who have left) and been a nuisance to neighbours.

We have now greatly improved our ability to identify those who are able to sustain their tenancy without support, i.e. behave and co-operate in claiming Housing Benefit. The net result is that we reject the majority of the unemployed who apply for accommodation with us. So think very carefully before housing the unemployed and find out how it works. I run for no charge to participants an HMO Academy where you can work in my business and learn the ropes. See my website www.hmodaddy.com for details.

46. **Question:** Jim, I am considering setting up an HMO to help house the homeless, which I feel is something worth doing. What do you think?

Answer: I applaud your sentiment, but appreciate that homeless people are not like you see in Christmas TV advertisements. Many people you see on the streets are not homeless they prefer to live on the streets just as some people prefer to live in caravans and boats. Others should not be called homeless it would be more correct to refer to them as 'home wreckers'. Some organisations make a very good living from the homeless due to the grants and donations they are given. Many charities get a lot of money by showing such people in a certain light. I am not criticizing this, I am pleased that society cares for those who are homeless due to misfortune. But not all is as it is made out to be.

I have tried to do my part and feel very privileged in being able to help homeless people by giving them accommodation but I do not want the home wreckers in my properties or in council speak 'those who are unable to sustain their tenancy without support'. I only want tenants who will act in a tenant like manner and it's important that you understand this if you're intending to let to this sector otherwise you could end up with empty wrecked properties. The rent arrears will be the least of your problems.

47. **Question:** I am having a problem with an unemployed tenant not paying their rent and stealing food from my other working tenants. What can I do?

Answer: Stealing is one of the problems with mixing working with unemployed. In effect there is legally nothing you can do with a bad unemployed tenant except evict them. You have all these charities complaining about poor homeless people, but many are homeless due to their own appalling behaviour. I feel a twisted kind of envy towards my unemployed tenants, as they can get away with almost anything, yet are considered deserving and entitled to all kinds of benefits. Conversely, I am treated with contempt in many circles, to be heavily taxed and punished. If you need further information on how to evict tenants, may I refer you to my manual 'DIY Eviction', only available at www.hmodaddy.com and my course on 'How to Evict a Tenant'.

48. **Question:** I took in someone who I thought was a nice person but was unemployed. He has now run off owing me over £1,200. What can I do?

Answer: When letting to the unemployed you are dealing with tenants who are not worth suing. They are also far more likely to sue you than working tenants! In short, there is no point suing the unemployed as they will not nor cannot pay even if you are successful in your action. All you will achieve is an unsatisfied county court judgment. Worse, if they sue you, you can rarely recover your costs, even if you successfully defend the action. Win or lose, you pay!

49. **Question:** My unemployed tenant has sold off all the furniture in the flat I rented to him and stripped all the copper pipe out, including the boiler, causing flood damage to the flat below. What can I do?

Answer: If an unemployed tenant does not pay their rent or damages your property then there are no consequences for their actions. Essentially, they are above the law, as if you sue them you will not recover anything. Even if you could show that the damage was deliberately caused or that they have stolen your goods, the police are unlikely to take any action. If they did, the penalties are often nominal. The most I have ever achieved using the police is to be awarded a Civil Restitution Order, which requires the tenant to repay the value of what they have taken with no penalty attached. This happened to me when a tenant stole a nearly new washing machine and fridge and they were even filmed on CCTV doing so. I am still waiting to be paid.

It gets worse. The tenants will often allege that their property was damaged by someone breaking in and stealing items and you must repair it. I have had tenants who, because they have lost their keys, break down the entrance door and then claim that it was done by someone else! Sometimes the council have assisted them with their demand that I repair the door.

50. **Question:** I housed in my HMO at the request of the homeless department, a rough sleeper who they said wanted to have a decent dry place to live. He was a charming man, but liked his alcohol, and left after about a month leaving the room in a disgusting state. I have seen him back on the streets. What is going on? Why did he leave the lovely room we gave him?

Answer: When you are a landlord dealing with the unemployed you must appreciate that certain people cannot be helped and you should avoid them. The paradox is that, in my experience, so does the very heavily subsidised social or voluntary sector. Yet they are paid so much exactly for providing accommodation for such people.

Social landlords have the ability to evict at will and do so. This means they can evict tenants from hostels and temporary housing without a court order, often immediately. Many of the homeless who apply to us for accommodation have been evicted from the social or voluntary sector. Once we had a relaxed attitude to taking such tenants. If we thought they would be ok, we would give them a chance and house them. We soon wised up! We suffered first-hand the problems they cause, so we are now much more selective. We rarely take those who have been evicted without a very thorough investigation as to the causes of their eviction. We also no longer believe what the council say about giving support or about the ability of the tenants to live unsupported, as the council officials have lied to us on too many occasions. They just want to get rid of their problems and happily dump them on the private sector.

I think you had a lucky escape as I have had homeless tenants who have caused a lot of damage to my properties. Console yourself with the thought that you gave someone a chance; you just do not know what demons they may be dealing with. Too many of the homeless are trapped on a downward spiral and some are keen to take as many as they can with them on their self-destructive journey.

51. **Question:** We do not normally let to the unemployed, but were considering letting to them. We were told by a friend, who is a social worker, that you are far more likely to be sued by such tenants. What is your experience Jim?

    Answer: Out of the 21 tenants who have tried to sue me over the last seven years, all but one was unemployed (and that one only worked part time). The highest proportion of unemployed tenants that I have housed, out of the 900 tenants I then housed, is 60% (i.e. 6 in 10 of my tenants at one time were unemployed and my long term average is less than 6%). This shows that the unemployed are a lot more litigious – it is not an equal relationship. Be very careful!

52. **Question:** A Housing Benefit officer has inspected some of my HMOs without my permission and told the tenants that the property does not comply with planning. He said the tenants are not entitled to the one-bed rate as they do not pay the council tax and the property is unfit for human habitation and he will get it closed down. It has recently been inspected by the Council's Housing Standards team and passed. What should I do?

Answer: You have identified a common problem where those who work in the Housing Benefit department interfere with matters that don't concern them.

Their job is only to administer Housing Benefit, not to police housing. Sometimes it is no bad thing when they do, but is always against the landlord. For example, if they know of a serial defaulting Housing Benefit tenant in the landlord's property, they never say a word, pleading data protection. Yet data protection does not seem to apply to reporting the landlord. The sheer hypocrisy of it annoys me.

I get around it by writing to the Housing Benefit department explaining that the payment of council tax and housing standards are not their concern. Housing Benefits must be paid to those over 35 years and sometimes, with a few exceptions, also to those under 35 at the one-bed rate where the tenant has exclusive use of sleeping facilities, cooking facilities, and bathroom. See my decision against Wolverhampton City Council as to what constitutes cooking facilities:

- A sink
- A fridge
- A microwave
- A kettle.

Housing benefit, Planning, Council Tax, and Housing Standards departments rarely work together. Even when they do, they soon fall out with each other. Just handle them one at a time. The rules they must apply are not integrated and it is the law they must follow, not what they would like to do (apart from Council Tax, they make it up as they go!) With Planning, they are concerned that you have turned each room into a flat, so if there's a shared fitted kitchen this usually satisfies them. They do not like to see a fitted cooker in the room. However, if within the rooms the cooking facilities are plugged in, i.e. a small cooker or microwave, kettle and fridge, they will usually lose interest as there is little they can do about it. Some landlords have been known to hide the cooking facilities in the rooms before the planners arrive or refer to them as tea-making facilities.

Housing Standards usually like to see cooking facilities in the rooms as they consider this is beneficial to the tenants and may even demand each room has a fridge and sink. However, if they do, they will usually insist on extra fire detection equipment (i.e. fire doors, heat detector in the room with cooking facilities and a stand-alone mains-operated smoke detector with hush button, plus an extractor fan for the cooking facilities). Some officers will also want to see the cooking facilities away from the door to the room in case there's a fire with the cooking facilities and this stops the tenants getting out of the room.

Licensing is unrelated to the above. You must apply what rules the Licencing Department say you must comply with. The licensing departments may or may not involve others, but as long as you have paid the fee and completed the form they are obliged to licence you (with only two very limited exceptions).

Oddly, being licenced seems to give your property the official stamp of approval. Once you have implemented the Licencing Department and Housing Standards' requirements, the planners tend to leave you alone, so there is value in being licensed!

Returning to your original question, should Housing Benefits not respond to your letter you must get the tenants to appeal, claiming the one-bed rate (and there's a time limit on this). Include photographs of the tenant in each room (the bathroom, cooking facilities and bed) as evidence. I once lost months of benefit because the tenant had stolen the microwave and I could not prove that I had supplied one. My word was not good enough, but the Housing Benefits officer's assertion that I had not was believed. This is the nonsense that you have to put up with.

CHAPTER 5
UTILITIES

Saving money on utilities is high on many HMO landlords' agenda. If anyone can tell me a practical way of providing heating without including 24/7 central heating within the rent, I would love to know.

53. **Question:** What does it cost to heat an HMO?

Answer: Analysis of my 140 HMOs shows it costs about £1,500 per annum to heat and provide hot water in an average HMO (4-8 tenants) using central heating. This is the cost when the heating is left on 24/7 and where I can set the thermostat at about 20 degrees. Even with some very old central heating systems that cannot be so controlled, it does not seem to make much difference. If I am very strict, and limit the heating to 20 degrees and have it on only for about 8 hours a day, I can reduce the cost to about £900 per annum. But I do not do this now as I feel it is not worth the time, effort and complaints that result. Restricting the heating could also bring you into conflict with the Housing Standards Department who often demand you provide 24/7 heating if you have agreed to provide heating within your rent.

I have discovered it costs the same to heat a four-bed HMO as to heat an eight-bed HMO. Sometimes, the larger HMO costs less than a smaller HMO! It makes no difference if the property is insulated (i.e. has wall insulation) or is solid brick, nor does the age of the boiler. Sometimes it's the reverse, and older, non-cavity wall houses cost less to heat even though the boilers are ancient, i.e. over 20 years old.

I shop around to find the cheapest gas supplier and I believe this is crucial and saves me more money than messing with central heating controls, as the cost of gas can vary by over 100%.

54. **Question:** I hear you provide unlimited central heating in your HMOs. Does it get abused?

Answer: Yes! I provide central heating in most of my properties and tenants rarely use the TRVs (thermostatic radiator valves) or the thermostat to control the heat but prefer to open the windows. It is a joke in my family that dad provides central heating so he can recognise his properties, as they are the ones with all the windows open, especially on the coldest days!

I have covered the issue of providing, or not providing, central heating in much more detail in 'Top Twelve Issues for HMO Landlords', only available from www.hmodaddy.com.

55. **Question:** Should I provide central heating in my HMO?

Answer: From a purely business point of view I cannot detect any benefit in giving tenants central heating unless the house is damp. Then, if it is not heated well, you will get mould problems which many believe wrongly are the landlord's responsibility. In fact, it is the reverse: you will save a lot of money and grief by not providing heating. If you do provide central heating, you will end up paying for it and when it breaks down tenants will be very critical and rarely appreciate that it can take time to repair. However, most properties will fail the EPC rating if central heating is not fitted and from 2018 you may not be able to let the property. This is easy to get around by fitting central heating, but telling tenants they have to pay for it themselves. Very few tenants will use the heating if they have to pay for it. For an EPC there is no requirement for the heating to be used!

However, not all my decisions are made on commercial grounds and I provide central heating in most of my HMOs as I think it is the right thing to do.

56. **Question:** Why should the landlord in an HMO have to provide a fixed form of heating?

Answer: It is the law! Landlords must provide fixed heaters (i.e. a heater screwed to the wall) but they do not have to pay for the heating. Some councils are demanding that it be an economical form of heating. I struggle to understand why an HMO landlord, or even a single-let landlord, has to provide heaters but does not have to provide furniture, which is also essential for occupation. Perversely, if the property is a single-let then the council would be unlikely to take any notice, as it is HMO landlords they like to pick on.

57. **Question:** How do I charge my tenants for heating my HMO?

Answer: Some landlords leave the tenants to sort out the bills between themselves, while others operate 'a fair usage policy' where they pay a certain amount and charge tenants for any overuse. With most of my tenants, this will not work. I have enough problems with getting them to pay their rent and they live mainly separate lives and do not interact with other tenants, so

I feel it is unfair or unreasonable to expect them to share expenses. If you do provide heating, then some councils demand that you provide 24/7 unlimited heating and give your tenants the ability to adjust the heat. You are not allowed to control or restrict the heating, so tenants just leave the heating on full blast and open the doors and windows to cool down.

So much depends on the attitude of your council and what is acceptable to both you and your tenants. Some councils are now muttering about providing economical heating and say ordinary electric heaters do not provide economical heating. They want you to provide gas central heating or electric storage heaters, which is nonsense, as my tenants will not use them if they have to pay for it.

58. **Question:** How do I know I am getting the best deal for my gas and electricity? There are so many offers that I cannot make out what is the best deal.

Answer: I agree. I suspect the companies deliberately make it confusing. The cost per unit is only part of the cost; you must also look at the standing charge. As HMOs tend to be high usage, it is best to go for the lowest charge per unit. Currently we are paying 3.89p per therm and 10p per day standing charge, and for electricity, we are paying 12.2p per kilowatt hour and 14.33p per day standing charge.

59. **Question:** What do you think of the various systems to automatically control heating in HMOs? I have seen systems where you can control the heating remotely, others which automatically switch off a radiator if the window is open, etc.?

Answer: Simple answer: I don't know as I have not used them. I have not used them because I believe (without any research) that they will save very little and so cost more than they are worth. The various systems have superficial appeal, but I suspect very strongly that they appeal to those who like to spend a pound to save a penny. No doubt, they are sold by slick salespeople without any reliable evidence as their effectiveness.

60. **Question:** What do you find the most cost-effective way of keeping your boilers up and working? Do you insure them so that when they break down, costs are covered?

Answer: We now only buy boilers with a long guarantee, which is currently seven years. How it works out, I'll let you know in a few years' time. The problem with boilers which only have a 12-month warranty is that they do not tell you about the other warranty they give for free, which is the guarantee that the boiler will not last more than 2 years! We do not insure the boilers as:

i. It is too expensive – you could buy a new boiler every other year for what the insurance costs!

ii. It is too much trouble getting the insurer to come and repair the boiler. We find it easier to use our own staff.

61. **Question:** What do you think of Hive? Should I install it? I am told you can save a lot of money by using it.

    Answer: I do not know whether Hive works. I appreciate that the assumption is that by switching off heating you are saving on gas, but how much more do you use when you switch the heating back on in heating the house back up? I appreciate that money-savingexpert.com says you'd be better switching it off (www.moneysavingexpert.com/utilities/energy-saving-myths#heatingon), but with HMOs I believe behaviour is different. As far as I know, no one has taken two similar HMOs which use the same amount of gas and tried using Hive on one of them and compared the saving. However, such a test would be unlikely to be a fair comparison. If they are occupied, then someone may leave the door open, run a bath, etc. It also depends on how you use Hive, how often you adjust the temperature or switch the heating off. This is the difficulty when it comes to testing anything that is said to conserve energy, as you are unable to replicate the same conditions so as to verify accurately if there are savings and if so, how much. It is often little more than a crude assessment or an act of faith – you just either believe you are saving money or not.

I remember hearing that switching an incandescent light bulb on and off produces no saving if it was on for less than 30 minutes because you use more electricity heating the bulb up, though I am not sure it is true. Maybe something similar applies to central heating.

Many years ago, I used to regularly visit my HMOs (often twice a day) and manually switch the heating on and off (a form of 'on-site Hive') and also faithfully read and recorded the utility meter readings every week. I went on holiday for two weeks over a very cold winter and came back to find the tenants in one of my properties had turned the heating on 24/7 and wound the thermostat up to maximum. I was mortified, until I read the meter!

By comparing the log of meter readings I had kept over the year, I found the property only used about 50% more than it did when I kept the thermostat low and had the heating only switched on for about eight hours a day. I was expecting the house to use over three times as much gas as the heating was on three times as long and at a much higher temperature. In fact, it only cost about half as much. In those days it cost about £800 per annum to heat my HMOs. Going on that one isolated incident, I surmised that if I left the heating on 24/7 it would cost about £1,200 per annum to heat the property. So was the £8 per week saving worth my effort, time and inconvenience to the tenants? No! I found the cost increase to be similar with my other properties. Since then I rarely interfere with the heating. I now leave the heating on 24/7 in most of my HMOs and still log the weekly usage.

Please let me know what your experiences are in using Hive, Nest, or similar. If I can save money without upsetting my tenants, I will.

To conclude, would you make a worthwhile saving considering the cost of Hive and your time in monitoring it and upsetting your tenants, as there is always one who wants the house heated 24/7? I somehow doubt it. Jim's rule is that common-sense does not apply with HMOs and being parsimonious does not go down well with tenants, so I have no intention at the moment of installing Hive.

62. **Question:** I have found in my credit file a default placed by a utility company for one of my HMOs, which I know nothing about. What can I do about this? Now, I can't get credit.

Answer: This is a common problem unfortunately and it is very difficult to get a default removed. My experience is that you have to sue the company to get the company to act. Prevention is better than cure and I recommend you do not put utilities in your name or address. Set up a separate business to handle all your utility bills to help avoid this problem in the future and be careful.

CHAPTER 6
HMO ISSUES

*This is a collection of questions that just don't
fit into any of the other chapters.*

63. **Question:** I am told that I should work **on** my property business not **in** my business, i.e. use an agent. What do you think?

    Answer: It's just hype. I can assure you that if you are local to your HMO it is much easier to do the job yourself (i.e. manage your business rather than get someone else to do it for you) and also far, far more profitable.

    If you employ others to manage properties that are only marginally profitable, you will end up losing money. For example, if you are 100% efficient then expect your staff or agent to be, at best, only 80% efficient. Model how your properties perform with only 80% of the rent and take out the letting agent fees from the bottom line. Can your business still work at that level of profitability? 80% is only a guess, so you must figure out the occupancy level below which each of your houses start to lose you money. Newbie property investors are usually highly leveraged (carry a lot of debts) and your profit is only a small percentage of the total income. An extra month's voids, bad debts or excessive costs wipe out all of your profit. Your staff will usually take more than twice as long to do the same work as you, and will often do it badly.

I have great difficulty in understanding the concept of people wanting to own buy-to-let property, but not be a landlord. It's a bit like being a footballer not wanting to play football, or being a teacher and not wanting to teach. It is insane and not good advice. If you want to have property, you should learn how to be a landlord, unless you like giving away most (or even all!) of your profit. You could even end up making a loss. It is not as if there is no help in being able to do this. I run my HMO Academy for free where you can train in my business by working with my staff (students attend without charge). Learn with the professionals! I also have a manual, which shows you how to operate an HMO business: see my 'Operating Standards for HMO Landlords' manual only available from www.hmodaddy.com.

By using a letting agent, you haemorrhage profits away in two ways:

The visible way is the percentage letting agents charge: normally 8% to 15%. Add to this the extras they charge for doing or arranging anything, such as getting gas certificates. They could charge £46 for something you could negotiate for £25 with no VAT. It may not seem much, but it all adds up.

The hidden and more insidious way is the lack of dedication to letting your property and collecting rent. The effect of any loss of rent or a void to a letting agent is comparatively minor: only 8% to 15% of the gross rent. Therefore, they cannot have the same motivation as you to be paid or stop the loss. However inadequate you feel you will be, you will be a lot more dedicated than a person who is paid to do the job. These agents are far more concerned with procedure in case you say they are negligent, while you will act faster and take a pragmatic view on say, a tenant who does not pass a credit check or does not have the deposit. If an agent does this, they could be considered negligent if the tenant does not pay or causes problems. An agent would rather play safe and leave the property empty than take a risk.

I appreciate that a newbie landlord may not know how

to be a landlord. What you do not know seems frightening to many and it is easy for me to say it will be okay. That is why I set up the 'HMO Academy' where people new to landlording are shown how to run an HMO by working in my business with those who are doing it. And they can experience it for themselves, so there are no excuses for not being able to do the job. See my website www.hmodaddy.com for details of the HMO Academy and it is for free!

Running a 6- to 8-bed HMO will take no longer on average than one hour a week, so you can run about 8 HMOs in one day a week. This includes interviewing tenants, checking the property, collecting rent, arranging repairs and all the administration that goes with running an HMO. I do not include the following in this time: maintenance, cleaning, redecoration etc. However, you could probably do most of that as well in not much more time if you had the skills, as a lot of time is spent in finding, supervising and organising tradespeople. Admittedly, you can make a mountain out of molehill and waste an inordinate amount of time on a job. I have staff that are very good at this! Conversely, armed with the right attitude, good organisational skills and the ability to multi-task, it is amazing just how much you can achieve.

The problem is you can rarely neatly fit all the time required to run an HMO into one morning, afternoon, evening or day. Most of the work can be grouped if you are very organised, but it is difficult. It is good to be available 24/7 for the odd emergencies (which may only happen once or twice a year) and to effectively manage your properties.

Being flexible with viewings enables your voids to be filled quicker. This means being available when your potential tenants want to view. My experience is that tenants rarely shop around and they take the first suitable property they find. If you are not available to view until Monday and it is Thursday, they are most likely to have found another property before then from a landlord who is prepared to work 24/7. Similarly, chasing bad-paying tenants takes time. Some tenants will avoid paying if they can get away with it and you need to be relentless to avoid high rent defaults. Similarly, with other matters (e.g. maintenance, etc.) a speedy response will work wonders for your business.

However, you can do what many letting agents do, which is close at 5pm and open at 10am. I know of a successful hands-on landlord who has a phone only available for tenants and turns his phone off at 4pm and does not switch it back on until after 10am the following morning. He has over 20 HMOs, and he and his wife do everything needed to run them, apart from certifying the gas, electric and fire alarm. They have numerous holidays and appear to have a fairly tranquil existence. It is not that hard to do and is also fun. The tenants' antics beat all the soaps on TV!

64. **Question:** The Council say that they want to send out a Housing Standards officer to inspect my excellent property – what will they be looking for?

    Answer: Don't worry, they will tell you. If your property is as good of a standard as you say, there are unlikely to be any consequences. However, they sometimes will do their best to find faults which they will ask you to rectify in order to justify the visit (and their existence!). Also, they will miss half of what you could be asked to do. I would wait and let them tell you what, if anything, they want. But make sure you do it or appeal if you don't agree. Do not ignore them.

65. **Question:** The Council have demanded that I fit programmable thermostatically-controlled electric heaters to my HMO rooms – must I do this?

    Answer: Yes! The landlord must provide a fixed form of heating in an HMO, but why the heaters have to be programmable I do not know. Programmable heaters cost in the region of £100 and you can pay a lot more. A simple heater with a thermostat will cost upwards of £15 and would be sufficient. They cost a fraction of the cost of programmable heater.

From my experience as a large HMO landlord with nearly 1,000 tenants, I very much doubt the tenants would use the programming part of the heater. Not only would I have difficulty in using the controls, but they also would confuse most of my tenants. I supply central heating in most of my HMOs and find very few tenants will use the TRVs (thermostatic control valves) on the radiator, preferring to open the window if it is too hot, or complain if it is not hot enough!

I suggest you reply in writing that you will fit electric heaters but ask why they have to be programmable, giving the reasons I have outlined and see if they agree. If not, you can appeal.

66. **Question:** I have recently successfully defended a prosecution brought against me by Housing Standards. Prosecuting me was totally unreasonable and the fault lay with the tenant. It cost me over £25k in legal fees to defend myself. What redress do I have? My barrister says that I should move on. What do you think Jim?

Answer: Yes, I agree with your barrister. You are unlikely to achieve anything by complaining to the council. But unfortunately, I have this stupid principle that you should strive for redress and/or make things better for other landlords. This is why I attend landlord committees until they invariably kick me out for telling them the truth.

I wouldn't let them get away with it. If there are no consequences what is to stop them doing it again? Perhaps I should believe the myth that what goes around comes around and unreasonable councils will be punished, and leave retribution to the gods!

67. **Question:** It is clear that a particular Housing Officer is out to get me. He has been very aggressive in his dealings and I suspect he is trying to get tenants to complain about me. What should I do?

Answer: Join the club! Nobody else will believe you as they do not appreciate it happens, or their experience has been that Housing Standard officers are helpful, professional and try to be fair. It is only when it happens to you that you realise what is going on elsewhere. So what do you do now?

I feel the best way to protect yourself is to go overboard in ensuring your properties are up to standard. I employ an ex Housing Standards officer as a part-time consultant to inspect and give written reports on my properties. It is not expensive to do – I pay mine £20 per hour and he does 6 to 10 HMOs a day (i.e. it costs £20 per HMO) and he inspects each HMO about every three months. This is in addition to the weekly inspections we make of our HMOs. Obviously, you must follow your consultant's recommendations and document them and your actions. Make sure your council knows you are using a consultant. Since I have started using one (I call him a Compliance Officer), the council I had problems with have laid off me. Whether it is because they know he works for me, I do not know. I get periods when a particular council takes an interest in me, and I get almost weekly dealings with them and then it dies down for months or years. If asked to do anything, especially if it is in writing or a notice is served on you, do what is required and do it quickly. Document and photograph that you have done the work. If you disagree with what is required or cannot comply in time, then you must appeal. DO NOT ignore the council's notices – do it or appeal!

Just in case they should try to prosecute you, ensure you have £10k to £30k in reserve to mount a robust legal defence. Learn how the system works. Say or admit nothing if invited for interview by your council, or if they caution you, until you have legal advice. Get a good lawyer who knows what they are doing with housing law and be resilient. Most landlords without good representation admit to offences that they should not have admitted to. They may not have done anything illegal, but often they cannot handle the stress of having a prosecution hanging over their head, so they take the pragmatic route and plead guilty. It usually costs far less to pay the fine than defending a case.

The only satisfaction you will have out of all this is that it will incur the council in the region of £100k to try to prosecute you if you defend. If they fail in their prosecution, questions will be asked of the officer, especially if they have been found to have wrongly prosecuted you. I have heard of a council officer who ended up on garden leave and 'retired' after an ill-conceived prosecution, but I think this is the exception.

68. **Question:** Something strange seems to be going on. I have just lost a good tenant who had a reasonable room and has now been re-housed by the council in a flat, and the day after the same council approached me to house a homeless person who turned out to have been recently released from prison for unmentionable offences. Why did the council not house him instead of my good tenant, as they are the ones who are supposed to provide housing for the so-called vulnerable?

Answer: At the vulnerable end of the market, private landlords and the social sector are competing for the same tenants, but the social sector gets paid an awful lot more for housing them (as much as ten times or more). Perversely, the councils who benefit from the extra funding are the ones who police the private sector they criticise. Yet they happily dump their problem tenants onto the private sector and it is never mentioned that the private sector houses the vulnerable at a fraction of the cost. Instead they emphasise how private landlords make money housing the vulnerable, yet fail to appreciate that landlords would not do it if they could not profit!

Thankfully there are many unemployed tenants who act in a reasonable way. Be warned however: if you allow a rogue into your HMO property it is akin to letting a fox into a hen house. A key landlord skill you must develop is being able to distinguish the decent unemployed tenant from the destructive degenerates.

69. **Question:** The sewers at my HMO keep getting blocked. As my HMO is at the end of the run, and presumably my tenants use the facilities more than the others, it is my HMO that suffers. I am fed up paying for the drains to be unblocked – it costs over £150 per time to call out the specialists. How do I get the neighbours to contribute?

Answer: Forget the neighbours – your local water company should be unblocking the sewer free of charge! If you have a shared sewer I believe it is the water company's responsibility (perhaps not if your house was built after 1930). Call them up and ask.

As for getting neighbours to contribute you could ask, but I doubt they will volunteer much sympathy or offer to share the cost. They may even reply that you have devalued their property by having an HMO in the area and it is your tenants who are blocking the sewers. After all, they could argue that if it was them, then the blockage would be further up the line. I know sewers do not necessarily work that way, but not many people understand how sewers work.

70. **Question:** A tenant is complaining that his room, and only his room, has been banded for Council Tax; yet I am still paying the Council Tax on the house, which has six bedsitting rooms, as an HMO. The council are getting two lots of tax. One lot of Council Tax from me and another lot from one of my tenants. What is going on?

Answer: Council Tax departments do not generally make any change without cause, so I suspect the tenant has contacted the Council Tax department and asked for his room to be separately banded.

I have had the same thing with some of my tenants (i.e. they ask for a Council Tax bill in their name). One of our tenants then went on to complain he was having to pay Council Tax while nobody else was. After considerable investigation, we eventually discovered that he had asked his Council Tax department why he was not paying Council Tax, so they obligingly agreed to charge him! He told them he had a flat in an HMO, when all he had was an en suite room with tea-making facilities and a kitchen he shared with everyone else in the house. When we discovered the truth, we asked the tenant why he did this and his reply was everyone had to pay Council Tax. So why he complained is a mystery.

When he left, we told the Council Tax department that he no longer lived in the HMO and the house was an HMO and did not have a flat in it. They very obligingly reassessed it back to a 'room' so now there is only the one Council Tax bill I pay on the house.

71. **Question:** My council has started an accreditation scheme for landlords where, if landlords agree to attend a course and act professionally, they can then be accredited. Do you think I should join?

Answer: I have mixed feelings. I believe that landlords should do everything they can do to show they act properly and within the law. Therefore, I have joined every scheme going and even made up my own landlord protocol, which provides a far better level of protection and service for my tenants than the heavily-subsided social sector. On the other hand, has it helped? I don't think so. I have never had a tenant say they had chosen us because we are accredited or a member of this or that. Further, I am not sure that drawing the attention of the council to you is of any benefit either. So, if you are the typical landlord who believes in doing nothing unless it has a direct financial benefit for them, I would not bother.

72. **Question:** I am thinking of creating an HMO in an Article 4 area. Is it possible to obtain from local authorities their opinion before I proceed with my application for planning permission?

Answer: The Permitted Development right to turn a house or a flat into an HMO for up to 6 people does not apply in an Article 4 area. You should apply for planning permission if you want to create an HMO in an Article 4 area.

Yes, you can ask the planners their opinion. The reply will probably be 'No chance' or 'When Hell freezes over'. They will give superficially plausible reasons for not allowing HMOs that do not stand up to analysis – there are very few legally justifiable reasons for not allowing HMOs.

Setting up an HMO in an Article 4 area requires a very subtle approach and be prepared for a long battle and to have to go to appeal. Unless you have unlimited resources to pay for planning consultants, you will need to do it yourself. You need to become an expert in this area of planning law and procedure, and be very robust with dealing with officials.

Alternatively, just sidestep the whole issue and operate either as:

i. Serviced Accommodation – what the difference in planning terms is between serviced accommodation and residential home and an HMO, nobody knows, so I doubt they will be able to do much with you if you say it is serviced accommodation! For more on this get my books Serviced Accommodation only available from www.hmodaddy.com.

ii. Let to a group of people of no more than six. As long as they live as a household it is not covered by Article 4 but is still an HMO. You must ensure they come as a group, have one agreement, and preferably there are no locks on the internal doors (except toilets/bathrooms) and they pay shared bills.

73. **Question:** I have approached my council asking if I can start an HMO in an Article 4 area in a large house near the town centre. It has been up for sale for a long time and I can get it at a good price. They have replied that an HMO would not be allowed due to the need for large houses for families, parking, lack of a garden in the proposed property and lack of room for refuse bins.

Answer: This is the typical nonsense that planners love to trot out. Superficially it sounds convincing, but when analysed it falls apart. For example:

• Where in planning law does it give priority to certain types of residential occupancy? Why should housing for large families take priority over accommodation for single workers?

- Is a large property near the town centre without a garden a 'family house'?

- Do families want to live near to the city centre? I doubt it – this is why the property is not selling!

- Where is the evidence to support that there is a need for large family houses compared to the need for HMOs?

- I suspect the large families want social housing (i.e. a council house), as the rent is usually cheaper and they have the right to buy at a discount. Stopping the use of private housing for HMOs is not going to remedy this.

- The requirement to provide parking near town centres or close to public transport has repeatedly been rejected by planning inspectors, yet planners continually bring this up when they know it will not be supported on appeal. This is a blatant abuse of the applicant's ignorance but keeps planning consultants in a job.

- The insufficiency of amenity space argument is probably their biggest own goal. Families with children are far more likely to need gardens, while very few HMO tenants use gardens.

- Refuse bins: this makes no sense; the same argument could be made for families. There is no evidence that HMOs need more bins than a large family. It is the management/responsibility that is the problem.

To start and survive in this business you need to be unafraid of authority, and be prepared to challenge the council and show enormous initiative. You will have to fight if you are to succeed in this business. Do not expect any support from your council even though you are providing low cost, flexible housing at a fraction of the cost of the social sector (which councils cannot now afford to provide). The reason, which is never raised in planning appeals, for the opposition to HMOs is class and racism. HMOs have traditionally housed the unemployed, vulnerable tenants and immigrants. HMO are one of the few areas where race and class discrimination can be practised.

74. **Question:** A property I am thinking of buying has a restrictive covenant saying it can only be used as one household. Will it cause a problem if I use it as an HMO?

Answer: I am not a lawyer – you should get proper legal advice.

My approach would be to ask: is the property leasehold or freehold? If it is freehold, if the entity that registered the restriction is no longer around to enforce it, you can take the risk and ignore it. If you are worried, ask your solicitor about insuring in the event of enforcement. Beware of breaching a leasehold covenant if you have an active freeholder who would seek to enforce the covenant.

75. **Question:** What are the implications of letting a property in poor decorative condition at a lower rent?

Answer: Be very careful as it can backfire! I did the same myself when I first started letting HMOs with a group of students who said they just wanted cheap accommodation. The property was luckily sound but in very poor decorative condition. Once in, the students started to complain and then the parents and college got involved. That I was only charging half the going rent made no difference – I was the slum landlord and the scheming students the victims!

I learned my lesson and thereafter always used to get a signed statement that the rent reduction was due to the decorative state of the property or whatever else. I now avoid doing anything like this at all. Though not illegal, providing the property is sound, I do not feel it is worth the risk to my reputation. Tenants who want something on the cheap quickly turn on you, and want a Rolls Royce service, conviently forgetting what they agreed and there are too many who are willing to fight their cause.

76. **Question:** I have had the council approach me over some flats I am turning into HMOs. Their building control officer says, as there are going to be more than 6 occupants in the block, I must soundproof between rooms and have the exterior walls insulated. Is this correct?

Answer: I have heard some HMO landlords have been asked to soundproof between rooms. It depends on how your building control officer interprets the legislation. Some treat rooms in an HMO as separate flats (therefore requiring sound proofing and insulation) while others treat them as rooms in a house. However, if you do not do as they require then you will not get a building control certificate to say that the works comply. They rarely enforce failure to complete, providing that you put in the building control application and pay the fee. Beware: this may cause problems later in getting finance if lenders ask for the relevant building control certificate.

77. **Question:** I recently applied for planning permission to convert my house into an HMO. One of the objections raised by the council is that there was no need for HMOs as the council provided accommodation. Why would the council say this?

Answer: Most likely because they are protecting their own interests. Some private landlords and the social sector are competing for the same tenants when housing the homeless and many of the tenants who claim Housing Benefit. Yet the social and voluntary sector get paid as much as ten times and sometimes more than private landlords receive. The councils mainly benefit from this extra funding, but they police and criticise those in the private sector. It is never mentioned by those who comment on housing that the private sector houses the homeless at a fraction of the cost that the social sector does, in the same or similar accommodation. The emphasis is that private landlords make money housing the vulnerable and provide poor standards. Yet they fail to appreciate that landlords would not do it if they did not make money. If surveyed, there is probably more poor housing in the social sector, but it is ok for the social sector to have poor housing because they do not have the money to do repairs.

78. **Question:** I had an unexpected visit from my Housing Standards department to one of my HMOs. They picked

up on a fault caused by a tenant and, without discussion or ability to defend myself, I received a written warning. Can I do anything about this?

Answer: This is very unusual behaviour. Usually councils ask you more than once to put things right. This council was out to get you. I would check that the council have followed their own procedure and if you have a right to appeal. If not complain or appeal though it is unlikely to achieve anything.

I had the same happen to me. After a mishap in one of my HMOs, I received a written warning without prior notification. However, when I asked a lawyer, I discovered it had no basis in law or legal significance and was a fabrication of the council. I had been given no right of representation or appeal, which goes against the fundamental principles of law that no action can be taken against a person without a right to a hearing and to an appeal process. The lawyers laughed at me for wanting to challenge the ruling. Yes, if I wanted to waste £10k to £50k they could get the formal warning quashed, as it was clearly unlawful and unjustified, but as it didn't mean anything, why bother? It seems injustice is the staple diet of our legal system.

I made a number of complaints to the council about their behaviour and even went to the Local Government

Ombudsmen without success. Is there no justice to be had? Here I am providing low cost, flexible, desperately-needed housing at a fraction of the cost (and often better quality) than the social sector, and far better than my competitors in the private sector. The problem is that the PRS is being judged by their subsidised competitors, the councils.

79. **Question:** With the tax changes, the tightening on lending, and large institutions now building to rent aided by billion pound grants from the government, do you think the party is now over for the amateur buy-to-let landlords?

Answer: Could be! So much has to do with luck, timing and area. Just as Purpose Built Student Accommodation (PBSA) in tower blocks/villages decimated some traditional private student landlords, the same may also apply to you. That there is change, and always has been, is not in dispute and the entrepreneur has to adapt. If I was in an area of rising house prices, then I would still be tempted to buy and rent. It may take a few years for demand to flatten and this will be the time to sell, cashing in on capital appreciation. It is a risk or gamble, but it has always been so. Those who can adapt will survive.

80. **Question:** I am considering buying a studio flat where I want to subdivide the lounge space into two separate rooms of 7 sq m each and let to two tenants. The property has a 100 year lease. Do I need permission either from authorities or the freehold owner?

Answer: I hate leasehold flats because:

i. Service charges are often extortionate.

ii. Bullying freeholders.

iii. The lease always says you must let the property to a family only, or words to that effect. I am unsure if this covers multi-lets.

iv. You need the freeholder's permission to carry out any alterations.

You may be caught by all of the above, but in particular by (3) & (4). Also, the council planning and building control departments may require permission. It would not be an HMO as there are only two tenants, and 7 sq m each should be okay (bedroom size is usually only a problem below 6.5 sq m).

My main concern is: Will it be profitable?

Two tenants, so double the rent, right? Wrong! You will be liable for their Council Tax unless you can make the tenants liable in the contract, but the ultimate liability for the council tax will rest with you. Then there is the problem over who pays the utility bills. This is similar to 2 + 2 model proposed by some for letting to those on Housing Benefit (i.e. two or more tenants over 35 sharing one property each with the sole use of two rooms are entitled to claim the higher one bedroom HB rate as opposed to the lower shared room rate). I found it did not work. It may be an area thing, but I doubt it. I haven't seen the occupancy rates of those who do 2 + 2s to assess their performance, but I don't trust the claimed success of this strategy.

81. **Question:** I have heard that they are planning to bring an Article 4 and additional licencing into my area. Should I be worried and what should I do?

Answer: I have an enormous moral dilemma over this. I run training courses to show newbie landlords how to become HMO landlords and can tell you from first-hand experience that what frightens them most is regulations. The dice are already heavily stacked against landlords with the one-sided eviction process, disrepair, Housing Benefit etc. The tenant can do no wrong – it is always the landlord's fault! More regulation, such as Article 4, Additional and Selective licencing schemes, just frighten off more landlords and this is what existing landlords want. Landlords hate competition.

Remember, HMOs are a product of housing shortage; they do not exist in areas of oversupply of housing. Encourage your council to bring in all it can and oppress landlords! Just make sure you are completely above board and meet all the licencing (Additional & Selective) and planning (Article 4) regulations.

There is also the added benefit that once you are inspected, you are in effect approved. It is like paying protection money. My experience of council inspections, which all licenced properties have to have, is that the inspectors are usually on the first visit friendly, courteous and miss 90% of what I worry about. Do as they say and you will have a clean bill of health (although I once had the council come back with a property I had recently taken over and had been inspected by the council six months previously when the owner looked after it. The council had not found any fault with the property when the owner ran it yet in my view it was substandard and unsafe and as a result I had to spend a lot in improving the property. Even though the property was substantially better on the second inspection the council found numerous things wrong with the property which clearly had been there six months previously along with faults I had already rectified.). That the property had been recently inspected by the council has been, I believe, a major factor in the successful defence of claims I've had from a growing number of tenants who have tried to sue me for alleged faults in the property, usually falling down or staggering upstairs.

82. **Question:** Can the council possibly refuse an HMO license given that the refurbishment standard meets their criteria, (e.g. fire doors, fire alarm, locks on bedroom doors etc.)?

Answer: A license can only be refused on two grounds:

i. **The property cannot be brought up to standard.** This I believe has happened only once and the tribunal overturned the decision on appeal. All the council can do is require you to bring the property up to standard and the standard is very variable depending which officer and council is inspecting the property.

ii. **You are not a fit and proper person to be a landlord.** This is invoked occasionally, but again you can appeal. It is time limited, not normally permanent, and easily circumvented by getting someone else to be the license holder.

All in all, the benefit of licensing is, from the authority's point of view, very little. It is all show, just to appease the baying anti-landlord masses that the council are being tough. It does allow the council to impose conditions on the license holder, but these can be challenged as I have successfully done. To break the license conditions is a criminal offence, although prosecutions are rare.

There are considerable benefits to being licensed, the main two are that commercial lenders prefer licensed HMOs and other council departments usually leave you alone once licensed.

83. **Question:** Planning permission has been granted in my areas for 180 flats to be built for rent and I am told more are on the way. Is it time for me to sell up?

Answer: I don't know. The institutions who are investing in these properties are either very clever or have little clue what they are doing. They would be welcome to some of my potential tenants, usually those I reject, but unfortunately a few get through! They would find their nice, new block stripped of every piece of metal and furniture overnight and turned into a drug den and/or brothel. Renting property is I believe not scalable, unless you are letting to professionals and I don't get many professionals applying for my accommodation, so maybe I am safe. These companies will only want to take tenants who fit a particular profile (i.e. working, possible to credit check and long term). The rest I suspect they will reject.

Yes, the market will change and no one is sure how. Maybe I am not the person to ask. There is a saying, 'There are those who make things happen, those who watch things happen and those who wonder what happened'. I am in the first and last category – whenever a new supermarket, fast food or coffee shop opens, I ask, "Where is the demand?" These places usually continue to survive, so they must have done their market research. However, I struggle with the concept of build-to-rent being the solution to the housing problem. Yes, there is a need, but I suspect it will be a bold experiment and, like purpose-built student housing, not cheap. Only a few years ago the council in my area were knocking down blocks of flats saying they couldn't rent them, so what has changed?

CHAPTER 7
PROSECUTING LANDLORDS

Rarely rational. Rarely fair. Rarely anything other than reflecting contempt for landlords.

84. **Question:** Do you think more should be done about prosecuting bad landlords?

Answer: I've yet to see any evidence or research that prosecuting landlords has any benefit. From what I have seen and anecdotal evidence, from the prosecutor's point of view, such legal action is expensive, time-consuming and gives an unsatisfactory result. Rarely is the level of penalty sufficient and they complain they don't recover the full costs of the action. How does the tenant benefit from a landlord being prosecuted? A likely outcome is the landlord selling up and displacing the tenants, who then will have to find other accommodation (which they should have done in the first place if the property was that bad)!

My investigation of landlord prosecutions shows is it arbitrarily imposed by some council officials with nothing better to do, or with an axe to grind. I defy you to find a shred of science, logic or rationality in any of it.

85. **Question:** What do you think councils should do with properties with tenants living in them which are in bad condition?

Answer: I am tempted to reply to this that the Council should get its own housing stock in order, but I believe you are referring to private landlords. My first question which is never answered is: why do tenants put up with the unsatisfactory conditions? I do not know. Why do they not move and be more selective over what properties they take? (I appreciate choice in some parts of the country is limited, so moving is sometimes not an option).

From a purely pragmatic point of view, it appears to me it would be easier and quicker for the council to remedy the defects themselves and get the tenant to deduct the cost from the rent. There is an established legal procedure for doing this, which Shelter (the homeless charity's website www.shelter.com) advocates – though the procedure could do with being simplified by removing the need for the tenant to get quotes. There you are, problem solved! And paid for by the landlord, without the need for enormous cost and time in trying to engage with the landlord, serve notices, and prosecute. Even the councils admit they rarely ever recover their costs in full when they prosecute!

And who is responsible for the defects? Many of the faults in my properties are caused by the tenants themselves. Yet, generally I must repair them. If the responsibility for repairs lay with the tenant or the council, the tenant would presumably have to pay for the repairs themselves.

Getting the work done and deducting it from the rent seems a generally satisfactory all-round solution. Most importantly, it gives a very quick fix for the tenants who are living in unsatisfactory conditions, as prosecutions take a long time and rarely address the harm that is being endured by the tenant. If the repair is down to the landlord, it is paid for by the landlord. Given that the landlords would have done the repair(s) far more cheaply themselves, they will be penalised for their incompetence or laziness.

86. **Question:** My council says they are going to ramp up their prosecution of landlords, but when I spoke to one of the Housing Standards officers they said it is unlikely to happen as it costs too much to prosecute. What is your take on this?

Answer: I have a suspicion that this drive to prosecute is more to do with someone wanting to make a name for themselves and/or a way for councils to generate income; the costs the courts award is more than sufficient to cover the prosecution. Although the fine is paid to the Treasury, the council can recover the court costs (around £3k), which seems to me excessive where there is a guilty plea (the Crown Prosecution Service can only recover £120 when the defendant pleads guilty in a magistrates' court). Where a council prosecutes a landlord, the costs awarded are at the discretion of the magistrates.

I knew a council official who was put in charge of a small council department. Her predecessor had taken one prosecution in 20 years. She brought twelve successful prosecutions in the first six months she was in the job and she did them all herself. She told me prosecuting was easy, you just fill in a form from the magistrates' court and job done! She was probably lucky in that all of her defendants pleaded guilty, as a defended case can cost the prosecutors tens of thousands of pounds in legal costs. I think questions would have been raised should a case have been defended and she had lost.

I was amazed that there was no strategy or control on prosecutions in her department or in the council; it was entirely down to the discretion of that one officer. They could do as they wished.

87. **Question:** Why do you say it is a waste of time to prosecute landlords?

Answer: Let's start with what will it achieve. The implicit assumption seems to be that it is a good thing to prosecute landlords, as it will teach those landlords a lesson and make them comply with the law and act as a deterrent to other landlords. I am wondering what evidence there is that prosecuting landlords has the desired effect on the landlord prosecuted? I know from my experience it puts a lot if decent people off from being a landlord.

As far as I can find there is no evidence or research available that prosecution of landlords is the best way to act or has any benefit. For my view, see question 84 above.

88. **Question:** What effect does being prosecuted have on landlords?

Answer: In my extensive experience of training HMO landlords, I see that fear of prosecution and regulations discourage a lot of newbie and single-let landlords from being HMO landlords. The few landlords I know who have been prosecuted were not bad people, nor had they committed some horrendous crime. Often, they did something that many HMO landlords do, but unfortunately for them, some official had arbitrarily decided to prosecute them. The experience of being prosecuted so embittered them that they sold up. So prosecuting landlords is a good thing for existing landlords, as it reduces competition and keeps rents high, unless they are the ones being victimised. My concern is that it is not the consistently bad or evil landlords who are prosecuted. The council pick easy targets who have just slipped up or are incompetent.

It seems that the general antagonism towards landlords is so deeply ingrained into our culture that nobody seems to question the notion of prosecuting landlords. Rarely are tenants prosecuted, yet in my experience they are the main cause of bad housing, either by neglect or by deliberate action in damaging the property or safety equipment.

89. **Question:** Surely bad landlords should be prosecuted?

Answer: For whose benefit? It should be reserved for the most extreme cases when all else fails and tenants are put at an unacceptable risk. Currently there is no sense of proportion; an unlucky, but otherwise good, landlord might find themselves in a council officer's sights merely to help them justify their existence. There but for the grace of God, go I.

90. **Question:** I have just read a report that my local council has prosecuted a landlord for not providing a fixed form of heating in their HMO for their tenants. I did not know that HMO landlords have to provide heaters – do they?

Answer: Yes, landlords have to provide a fixed form of heating in an HMO – portable heaters will not do. However, you don't have to pay for heating, just supply a fixed form of heating. In my experience, the tenant will rarely use it if they have to pay. The report you refer to involved a house with three bedsits, where the tenants were living in damp and cold conditions with unsatisfactory heating. Why was this the landlord's fault? Lots of people live in cold conditions because they chose not to heat the property and the damp was probably the result of not heating or ventilating the property properly. Still, it is far better than living on the streets. The council issued an improvement notice requiring the landlord to install programmable fixed heaters to each bedsit, which the owner failed to do in time. I have little sympathy for him. If you are served with a notice either do it or appeal against it. Though I do not think much of such action by the council, it is not a good idea to ignore them when it gets to this stage.

A programmable electric heater can be purchased for less than £100, so, with fitting costs, I estimate the total cost would be less than £500. The owner was fined £2,000 for failing to comply with the notice. The prosecution costs were, according to the council, an unbelievable £2,915 for which they recovered £2,140 (a shortfall of £775), and it took over nine months for the heaters to be fitted. I fail to see why it costs nearly £3,000 to prosecute the landlord – a criminal prosecution where the defendants plead guilty is not that complicated and probably involves less than 10 hours of work.

To me, the most satisfactory course would have been for the council to encourage the tenants to buy the heaters themselves by taking the cost of the heaters out of the rent or to have had the work done themselves and charged the landlord. The matter could have been simply resolved in days, without cost to the council, as it would be paid for by the landlord. In time and effort, it would have been cheaper for the council to have fitted the heaters themselves.

I suspect that the tenants would not use the electric heaters if they were paying for the electric bill themselves, as they either could not afford to do so or would have chosen to spend their money elsewhere.

Whichever the case, the 'harm' that is being addressed would not be remedied – i.e. the cold and damp conditions would remain. Electric heaters are not that expensive. They can be obtained for less than £10 and if the tenants were going to use them, they would have bought some, so I believe the whole prosecution process will have turned out to be a waste of time.

91. **Question:** My council has just announced a crackdown on rogue landlords and has obtained funds from central government to enable it to prosecute more landlords. It is making me think twice about investing in property in my area. Should I be worried?

   Answer: I am not sure. Many local landlords will be breathing a sigh of relief to hear that their council's crackdown is putting off potentially good landlords, such as you and others who are concerned about their legal obligations, and this is the problem. All I think that these so-called crackdowns do is put off good conscientious people being HMO landlords. Rarely do they catch the evil ones and action is often taken against landlords who are at least no worse, and sometimes much better, than many others.

CHAPTER 8
FUNDING & SOURCING PROPERTIES

Money.
Despite what anyone may tell you, it helps.

92. **Question:** How do you think the new laws will affect property investors and how can I, a newbie, still invest and make money in property? Is there a new strategy to follow?

Answer: By the new laws, I assume you are referring to the limiting of mortgage interest relief to basic rate tax for individual buy-to-let borrowers. The implications have yet to be thought through, but the general feeling is that property owners now need to operate as limited companies. All new purchases should be via a limited company to enable mortgage interest to be treated fully as an expense. Buying via a limited company should not make that much difference to a property investor's ambitions.

93. **Question:** Do you source and fully manage HMOs for clients?

Answer: I have just started to source HMOs in my area which I will then manage for the owner, as well as JV'ing and sharing the profits. I charge from £10k to find HMOs (depending on the size) and I guarantee you will get at least all of your money back on mortgaging.

To manage the building work, I use my own builders, for which I charge a management fee. However, even with this extra charge you will still get all your money back on re-mortgaging.

We will manage the property for 15% of the gross rent. This covers finding tenants, managing them, collecting rent, checking the property and ensuring the property is fully HMO regulation compliant. Minor repairs are charged at £200 per unit per annum. This saves administration in tracking and itemizing every minor job.

You are free to choose to use all or any part of the above services, or to try and do it yourself, and I will take over if it goes wrong.

94. **Question:** How do I know I can get finance for my HMO if I JV with you?

    Answer: Usually, this question is followed with: "...at my age? I don't have steady or any employment or I am not a property owner."

    Everyone who I have helped JV has got finance regardless of age, employment or property status. It is easy to check out – I direct you to the appropriate lender and you ask for a DIP (Decision In Principle). Though this is not legally binding, I have never known a lender refuse to lend after a DIP.

95. **Question:** If I joint venture with you after I have bought my HMO with your help, will I get all my money back out?

    Answer: I always say there are no guarantees, although everyone I know who wants to has always got all their money back out. Sometimes it may take two applications to lenders to achieve this, but it has always worked. When JV'ing with me, my fall-back guarantee is that you keep 100% of the net profit until you are re-paid in full out of the profit.

To summarise, the options are:

i. Re-mortgage until the investor's initial input capital is fully recovered (and maybe more). This may take more than one mortgage application and may mean changing lenders. The downside of recovering all your capital is a lower, long-term income (profit) from the property due to higher mortgage payments.

ii. Recover none or part of the investor's initial input capital. The agreement provides that all the net profit will be paid to the investors and treated as repayment of initial capital and costs without interest until the investor is fully repaid. Should the JV investor decide on this course of action, then no profit will be payable to either JV partner. I have an anti-abuse rule that if the JV investor fails to apply for a mortgage or to re-mortgage until all of their input capital is recovered (and keeps the surplus income), then the reduced management fee I charge will increase to cover the true cost of managing an HMO, until a profit share is made.

96. **Question:** Do mortgage companies ever call mortgages in? If so what happens?

    Answer: Yes, lenders have been known to do this, usually only with commercial loans. They can always find some technical reason to call in the loan, such as breach of the Loan to Value (LTV) covenant. This happened after the crash and a lot of developers went bust, when the banks called in their loans. I have been threatened by the banks in the past and had to agree to amended terms, such as an increase in the margin payable.

The old saying that banks will lend umbrellas when it is sunny and call them in when it is rainy is only too true. However, if you worried about what could happen, you would never do anything. If it is a concern, then limit your liability by only borrowing using a company and do not give a personal guarantee. This may severely limit your ability to borrow and increase costs. We all take risks according to how we assess them or those we feel comfortable with.

97. **Question:** I have a property which I wish to buy and turn into an HMO. I am unsure whether to go for a buy-to-let mortgage or a commercial mortgage?

Answer: I am not a mortgage broker so I am unable to give advice, only information, and I only deal with commercial mortgages myself. However, from what I hear with both types of lending, you need a good credit history but commercial lenders are far less fussy. With commercial lenders, having an unsatisfied CCJ seems to be the only thing that is fatal. Generally they have a wider discretion to lend than buy-to-let lenders. Buy-to-let lenders only lend on the value of the building based on its 'bricks and mortar' value (i.e. what it is worth as a house) and will generally need the rent to be about 150% of the mortgage payments. Buy-to-let lenders also tend to be much fussier about the condition of the property and want you to have a minimum income in the region of £25k.

With commercial mortgages you do not need an income, although it helps if you do, as it makes you more attractive to the lender. The loans are usually based on the property itself and I have even had lenders say to me that they lend purely on the proposition, which is the income-producing property. They will not generally lend on property unless it is producing income. However, a number of commercial lenders will do what they call 'development loans', where they lend on the potential income.

Once the property is producing an income (i.e. you have bought and let it), commercial lenders generally want you to have at least 30% invested, plus an income which covers the mortgage interest and capital at about 200%. In other words, the gross rent must be around twice the mortgage payments. Some lenders are more relaxed and will lend up to 70% of the investment value regardless of what you have spent.

Crucially, commercial lenders will only lend to

experienced landlords, but will often take into account your support network if it is sufficiently qualified. Having the right contacts is an enormous help. Commercial lenders are also usually far more expensive than buy-to-let mortgages, both in the interest rate margin and fees. Contrary to popular belief, you can get commercial lending on a house or flat based on income, provided it is clearly adapted (i.e. Has fire doors and a fire alarm) and it helps if the property is licensed.

98. **Question:** As HMOs can be valued on income can I increase the value of my HMO by increasing the rent, by say, including free gym membership in the rent?

Answer: Good idea, but unfortunately it may not work as valuers also assess whether the rents charged are reasonable for the area and property, and some can be very negative and down-value the rent you charge. They may deduct from the rent any extras, such as utilities and your gym membership. I have had valuers down-value by 30%, saying I was getting a 'rack rent'. They compared my rents to the shared house rate paid by Housing Benefit. I was renting en suite rooms with kitchenettes which would have attracted the one-bed rate if let to Housing Benefit tenants. It goes to show that valuers get it wrong. I was at the time under-charging, as all the tenants worked for the same company and I did a deal with the company owner.

The problem is that when you do not get the value you need, it can destroy the deal. It is one of the many risks you take, and an expensive one at that. There is no certainty in this process. I have done it over 100 times with about 80% success. So even I am not 100% successful. As Robert the Bruce (the famous Scottish king) is reputed to have told his troops, 'If at first you don't succeed try, try and try again'. Beware, having to find another mortgage takes time and cost.

99. **Question:** How do commercial valuers value an HMO?

Answer: The simple answer is, as they want! Ask ten different valuers and you will get eleven very different valuations on the same HMO. I have had valuations of more than double what another valuer said it was worth. I obviously binned the low valuation when I went to the bank for a loan!

Valuers will say they have rules to follow, but from my observation, valuers take two approaches:

i. 'A common sense' approach. Such surveyors usually say they are 'very professional' and the resulting valuation is usually very low. They refuse to value the HMO on income, but as a house, but still charge a commercial valuer's fee. Another trick is to ask what you paid for the property and then value it at that figure, saying this represents the market price! I never use such valuers if I can avoid them.

ii. 'Based on comparables'. This valuer will look to see what other HMO properties in the area have recently sold for, usually in auction. The report will list these comparables, saying for example:

- HMO X sold for £500k which represents 10x gross annual income of £50k

- HMO Y sold for £1.2m which represents 12x gross annual income of £100k

- HMO Z sold for £750k which represents 16x gross annual income of £47k

The strange thing is that when they decide the value of my HMO, they say they will apply a multiple of about 8! I would argue that the average in the above comparables was nearer 13 times income. Further, they should add 25% as they are using auction comparables. Typically, properties achieve only 80% of market value at auction in return for a quick and certain sale.

Worse, some valuers say your rent is too high and reduce it, or deduct a figure for expenses. Such deductions can be a straight percentage figure (10%-

40%) or a detailed analysis of costs i.e. gas, electric, water, insurance, and management, etc. Occasionally, they may also deduct a figure for voids. I had one valuer who deducted 25% and the utility costs. Occasionally, a valuer will also deduct the cost of selling. None of this makes any sense, as they do not apply these adjustments to the comparable sold prices of HMOs on which they based the initial value.

To add insult to injury, I have had valuers refuse to confirm the valuation or flag up a problem. The usual problems are lack of planning, lack of building control, movement in the property, no or low EPC rating and HMO licencing issues. Then the lender will refuse to lend on the property, which could be because the property does not have building control approval for works carried out years ago. The lender may accept indemnity insurance in such a case. I've asked the obvious question of whether the auction comparables they started off with had these issues. You bet no notice was taken. I have never seen a building control completion certificate notice in an auction pack!

Essentially, much in property makes very little sense, especially HMOs. There is little science to it and it relies too much on luck. However, over the long term you have a much better chance of success than playing the lottery!

100. **Question:** I have had an awful year, and some of the HMOs I am planning to re-mortgage have performed very badly. When valuers value an HMO on income, do they take into account actual rent received or the potential rents?

Answer: All the valuations I have had done have always been based on potential rents (i.e. gross rents charged). Nothing to do with rents received. I would NOT mention your problems to the valuer as he may down-value the property. Yes, I know this does not make any sense! Don't worry, it works and it is to your benefit.

101. **Question:** What should I budget for voids and bad debts when doing my calculations of profitability?

Answer: I am not sure. According to RLA Media Review 22.04.16, the average rent arrears are 9.3%.

This figure is a lot more than my current experience, but during the recession my arrears were a lot worse than this. Most of my fellow landlords deny having rent arrears. I have heard that HMRC will accept rent receipts of 80% of the total potential income, suggesting they think HMOs average 20% bad debts and voids.

How do I reconcile my experience and the statistics with what my fellow landlords say? No one wants to admit their failures, so I believe they people will understate information or put a different spin on information that is harmful or damaging to them. Therefore, it is to be expected that landlords would understate their bad debts. They worry that people will think they are incompetent in tolerating such poor performance – why can't they do better? The same happened with the amount of alcohol people say they drink when asked by a doctor, as it makes them look bad. Research shows it is understated by well over half. People drink twice as much as they say they drink!

Another problem is that over 90% of the population are innumerate. To help this majority, this means nine out of ten people have difficulty with arithmetic! They simply cannot calculate what bad debts they have as a percentage. This is a truly appalling reflection on our education system, but mainly down to the individual as I believe it is our own responsibility to be educated. Another reason is down to lack of analysis. We are not calculating machines, but emotional beings and we operate on feelings, not statistics. Keeping records is time-consuming and not exciting.

I am also fairly confident that voids vary around the country and properties let quickly in areas of high demand. My experience is that well-prepared studios (rooms with en suites and kitchenettes) let quicker than rooms and that dressing a room helps a lot in getting them let quickly.

THE END!

MASTER HMO'S TODAY,
CHANGE YOUR LIFE
FOREVER

BOOKS

MANUALS

COURSES

MENTORSHIPS

AND CONSULTANCY

AVAILABLE FROM HMO DADDY

at WWW.HMODADDY.COM

BOOKS

HMO Landlord Rules - £4.97

Downloadable Version - £1.97

Written by an HMO landlord with 20 years' experience, this small, frank and helpful guide looks at exactly what works and what doesn't when managing properties. Instilled with a strong sense of evidence and proof, he exposes some widely-accepted claims as rubbish or a con. The aim is to ensure maximum income for minimum work. It includes helpful information such as: • How to pick good tenants and get rid of bad ones • Whether to believe non-payment excuses • When to give something for free and when to charge • When to serve notice on a tenant • How to deal with abandonment and late payments • How to avoid litigation • and much more! A set of rules, principles and structure for all HMO Landlords.

HMO Daddy Reveals All - £19.99 (Published April 2017)

Downloadable Version - £14.99

Jim Haliburton (HMO Daddy) reveals all in this easy-to-read, comprehensive guide. The publication details Jim`s extensive knowledge on all aspects of the HMO market. Aimed at both existing HMO landlords and those who are thinking about entering the market alike, Jim discusses the problems and issues surrounding, what can be a complex investment.

This HMO business can be a lonely road with seemingly no one to turn to or able to understand the problems we encounter – Jim's guide helps investors through these difficulties with this much-needed clarity and candour, as is Jim's inimitable style.

101 Questions and Answers Relating to HMOs - £9.97

Downloadable Version - £6.93

All the questions you wanted answers to, and some you had not even thought about. Jim Haliburton, also known as the HMO Daddy, has compiled the answers to the questions he has been asked. There is an enormous thirst for knowledge about HMOs from existing HMO landlords and those thinking of entering the business and HMO Daddy has not shirked away from answering even the most difficult of them. A must-read for all those who have HMOs or are thinking about becoming an HMO landlord.

More 101 Questions and Answers Relating to HMOs - £9.97

Downloadable Version - £6.93

In this book, Jim Haliburton answers even more of the essential questions you wanted to know about HMOs, including his personal property journey, how to get started on your HMO journey, potential tenant Issues, how to let to the unemployed or homeless, dealing with utilities, handling general HMO issues, matters regarding the authorities prosecuting landlords and HMO funding techniques.

35 Money-Making or Saving Tips for HMO Landlords - £9.97

Downloadable Version - £6.93

Written by an experienced HMO landlord, this is an insider's guide to creating extra income and savings from your property portfolio. It includes information to help you make savings on repairs, maintenance and decoration of your properties. It includes tried and tested tips used by the author himself, and includes information on creating extra rooms in your properties, introducing and charging extra fees and top-ups, fitting master locks and electric meters, making savings on light fittings, repairs and decoration. It explains which services can be charged for and which should be free, as well as how and when to introduce new fees without upsetting your tenants. If you're an HMO landlord, this will give you a frank and honest way to maximise the returns on your property. Just applying FIVE of the tips to four of your HMOs will give you the PROFIT of an EXTRA HMO.

Planning & HMOs - £9.97

Downloadable Version - £6.93

IIMO landlords provide low-cost flexible housing desperately needed by society, often to vulnerable tenants. However, they are rarely given help or support by the authorities, and the law is often vigorously enforced against them. Little is said about the damage some tenants cause to property, problems with rent arrears and eviction of bad tenants. This book is for the brave souls who dare to provide HMO housing and need a guide to the planning system. It shows you how to stand up to councils that try to stop you providing good quality HMO accommodation. If you stand up to the planners, you will be surprised how rarely they will follow through and how often they will lose. A unique insight, and practical information about planning rules and planning appeals for shared houses and multi-lets, by an experienced HMO Landlord.

HMO & Compensation for Unlawful Eviction - £9.97

Downloadable Version - £6.93

This practical, down-to-earth guide is written by HMO Daddy, an experienced landlord who had a case brought against him for unlawful eviction by an HMO tenant. When he got to court, he realised he was looking at a possible compensation claim of around £100,000. With no experience in this area, he could find little guidance or help to explain the system. He won his case – but this is the book he wishes he'd had at the time! This quick and easy-to-understand guide examines court reports and cases involving unlawful eviction along with the amount of compensation awarded. It brings home to landlords, the seriousness of the risks they are taking when evicting tenants and more importantly it explains how to avoid ending up in court.

A Compendium of HMO Daddy's Blogs - £4.97 Self-Published

Downloadable Version - £1.93

This collection of invaluable HMO advice and tips, shared by Jim Haliburton, covers tips for new investors into HMOs, costly mistakes to avoid, how to become a successful HMO investor, what makes a property investor different from a general investors, how to avoid LHA claims, unusual properties bought, how to evict unemployed tenants who refuse to pay and what is wrong with current housing standards.

Current Issues for HMO Landlords - £9.97 Self-Published

Downloadable Version - £6.93

Current issues for HMO Landlords looks at the twelve pressing issues in detail, that landlords or property investors frequently ask about. These include: which properties let and which ones do not; whether to use AST or licenses for HMOs; how to keep tenants; assessing rent-to-rent; getting commercial finance; when to fix and when not to fix a mortgage; how to save money on heating; when to use letting agents and when not; as well as how to identify the need for HMOs.

Introduction to Letting to the Unemployed £9.97 Self-published

Downloadable Version - £6.93

This is probably the most heartfelt book I have ever written as it deals with homelessness and I have been homeless myself when I left care as a child. I have given numerous copies away to the lovely people I meet who tell me they want to start an HMO to house the homeless, women who have been domestically abused and the likes. Please read it before you start to let to the unemployed and I applaud and will help you if you decide to go ahead.

HMO Daddy

Serviced Accommodation - £9.97 Self-Published

Downloadable Version - £6.93

This book is an outline of the legalities involved in operating as Serviced Accommodation. I wrote this because when I first considered using some as my properties for Serviced Accommodation, I could not find any information on the subject. I, therefore, researched the topic and have come up with this book.

HMO Daddy

Employing an HMO Manager (to be published end of 2017)

Jim Haliburton, known as the HMO Daddy, outlines the process for and nuances in employing a property manager to help efficiently run, systemise and scale the process of running your HMO portfolio.

**To order any book or books please visit
www.hmodaddy.com**

MANUALS

How to Become a Multi-Millionaire HMO Landlord - £597

Downloadable Version - £497

Written by an experienced HMO landlord, with 140 properties and nearly 1000 rooms. Originally written in 2005 and updated regularly, this manual has stood the test of time and is the authoritative guide to starting and setting up an HMO. The manual shows how HMO Daddy started and runs his HMOs and how you can do the same. It covers the HMO market; acquiring the ideal property for an HMO; negotiating the right price; tenant selection; property management; property standards and general advice on property. The 'How To Become a Multi-Millionaire HMO Landlord' manual will help novice or experienced single-let landlords transform their property portfolios into profitable multi-million cash-flowing assets. A complete how-to guide in one manual.

DIY Eviction - £125

Downloadable Version - £99

Jim Haliburton (HMO Daddy) clearly explains using his experience of evicting over 300 tenants through the courts with 100% success, and far more tenants without having to go court to evict. He shows that by using the correct legal process it is possible to evict a problem tenant without the necessity of using a lawyer. This is the only DIY guide to evicting tenants and simply explains how to evict tenants and, if they refuse to go, how to use the legal process to successfully remove a tenant from your property cheaply, quickly and legally. The guide tells you how to answer all the questions ever asked of Jim by judges in the eviction process and how to deal with matters when the eviction goes wrong. It is recommended you buy this along with my book 'HMOs and Compensation for Unlawful Eviction' (see book section).

Operating Standards - £297

Downloadable Version - £197

'Operating Standards' contains all the knowledge, the scripts, the tools and the systems to run your HMO portfolio with clear step-by-step processes to manage any potential HMO issues.

The thought of starting or running an HMO portfolio can be very daunting as you do not know whose advice you can trust, how to get the legals right letting to tenants and inspecting properties.

'Operating Standards' contains all the information you need

to run your HMO and consistently build your income. This includes: customer care, letting criteria and arranging interviews, answering the telephone to prospective clients, showing premises, handing over premises, tenant rating, repairs and tenant requests, dealing with tenants, dealing with local housing allowance (LHA) claimants, dealing with late-paying tenants, collection of rents and dealing with building works and renovations.

Implementing the Operating Standards has the potential to replace your salary in 12 months and contains plans and checklists to help you run your HMO efficiently and profitably or show staff how to do it.

'Forms, Notices and Agreements' Manual, With Memory Stick –£225.00

Downloadable Version - £125

The Forms, Notices and Agreements manual covers all the relevant forms including: application forms for tenants, tenancy pack, abandonment documentation, ASTs, court forms and assorted notices for tenants including Section 8 Ground 8, 10 & 11 for landlords – 65 different forms, notices and agreements at the last count.

These forms, lists, notices and agreements are essential paperwork that all beginner or established landlords must have to run their property portfolios legally, efficiently and profitably.

To order a manual or manuals please visit:
www.hmodaddy.com

MASTER HMO'S TODAY, CHANGE YOUR LIFE **FOREVER**

COURSES

Tour of HMOs - £297 One-Day Course

Our famous Tour of HMOs day is a behind-the-scenes look at how Jim Haliburton sets up and runs his HMOs. The day will give you an incredible insight into how you can maximise profit whilst still offering the very best in tenant care and safety! Jim houses over 1000 tenants and has all types of properties throughout the West Midlands area.

During your one-day course, you will be taken to visit several different HMOs including two-bedroom and three-bedroom terraced or semi-detached houses that are now five- or six-bed HMOs.

You will be shown how to maximise the income from a typical single-let from a gross of **£550 pcm** to a phenomenal **£3120 pcm** gross from the same property converted to an HMO, all legally and ethically.

Come and learn from over 26 years of property investing experience how I acquire, set up, convert, refurbish and manage the 140 HMOs in my portfolio, with in excess of 900 rooms and still counting.

Whether you are an experienced property investor or are thinking about investing in property, HMO investment is definitely the way to maximise your rental returns. Over 2,500 people have now attended HMO Daddy's Tour of HMOs – probably the most popular HMO course ever!

Come and see first-hand exactly what an HMO is by visiting several of my HMOs with me.

The course includes:

- All the course materials and slides.
- Expert tuition with the HMO Daddy team.
- Transport to and from the HMOs - we aim to visit up to three properties in various stages of conversion.
- Lunch.
- Tea and coffee breaks.
- Overnight stay in one of HMO Daddy's HMOs (subject to pre booking and availability).

Commercial to Residential £1997 Two Day Course

In every town in the UK there are old, empty, unloved units gathering dust. Have you ever looked and thought, "I wonder if I could turn that giant building into profit somehow?"

You can and we want to show you how, right away how to acquire such a property for £1 or less, and how to finance so that you can obtain and recover all you spend on the property so you do NOT NEED MONEY to acquire such properties.

Covering all the legislation and conversion considerations you must know, we also take a tour of several converted premises to show you what we have done and that you can do too.

Our unique training programme will provide you with a chance to make great profit through converting commercial property into cash-flowing residential developments. It takes you through a step-by-step process and shows you how to take control of empty commercial property with little or no money at all and convert them into profitable residential premises.

This course will cover, among other things, how to easily identify commercial to residential conversion opportunities, understand planning laws and loopholes, putting your team together as well as getting other people to fund the conversion process if required.

Rent-to-Rent - £397 One-Day Course

Do you know the difference between a rent-to-rent deal, a rent-to-buy deal, a lease option, an instalment contract, and an exchange with delayed completion?

Perhaps you have heard these terms bandied around the industry for a few years, but you have not yet found anyone that can clarify the difference and really show you which of these strategies is right for you?

This is where I come in. There are very subtle differences in these strategies, but all of them are within reach for you even if you have very little capital to invest – as shown by HMO Daddy who walks the talk and has over 30 rent-to-rents.

This introduction is perfect for you if you are starting out on your rent-to-rent journey.

Learn the basics of deal sourcing and negotiation. The course provides you with the paperwork to go out and immediately do rent-to-rent contracts.

Come armed and ready to develop your understanding of rent-to-rent. Discover how you can kick-start your rent-to-rent business straight away.

For a small investment of just £397 (no VAT) you can join us with a guest FREE OF CHARGE and kick-start your journey to financial freedom.

The HMO Success Formula - £1997 Two-Day Course

This two-day course provides a step-by-step guide on how to become an HMO landlord, whether you are a novice or an experienced landlord.

Designed by Jim Haliburton, the HMO Daddy, this course covers all the relevant information required to enable you succeed in setting up and efficiently running your portfolio of HMO properties for great profit. It includes comprehensive course notes.

COURSE CONTENT

Income from HMOs

What Is an HMO

HMO Licencing

HMO Myths

Objection to HMOs

How HMOs Are Valued

Different Models of HMOs

Different Models of HMOs

HMO Hot Spots

Finding Tenants

Attracting Tenants

Managing HMOs

Interviewing Tenants

Planning

Keeping Tenants

Council Tax

HMO Strategies including:

Utility Costs – How To Reduce and Avoid

Buying

Tenant Issues

Rent-to-Rent

Building Control

Delayed Completion

Housing Standards

Vendor Finance

Conversion Costs

Leases

Com to Resi

Adverse Possession

With all courses, you can stay on HMO Daddy's HMO rooms for a nominal charge subject to availability and prior booking

The courses are usually held at our training suite in Walsall

To book a course or courses please go to: www.hmodaddy.com

MASTER HMO'S TODAY,
CHANGE YOUR LIFE
FOREVER

MENTORSHIPS

HMO Academy

Work as an HMO Landlord - No Charge

The HMO Academy 400-hour internship. Come to us in Walsall for 400 hours over about six months, (an average of a couple of days per week), or you can do it all in one go, which should take you around eight weeks. You choose how you want to do it. Shadowing every department of our lettings company, you get a chance to assist with tenant interviews, viewings, rent collection, maintenance, and house conversion, and also spend time with the HMO Daddy training team, acquiring new properties and planning their conversion.

By attending the HMO Daddy Academy, you will receive the extensive course manual and our operating standards, which you are expected to read and understand. You will learn all the techniques you need to run your own portfolio and spend a lot of quality time with Jim Haliburton and the team. In return, we ask you to work as requested in the various departments and bring whatever skills you have to the business. To apply, we ask for your CV or summary of you and what you have done, some personal details and a deposit of £1,200. When you complete the 400 hours, we return the £1,200 deposit. Free accommodation is available.

HMO Daddy offers limited bursaries for the above. If you are unable to afford the £1,200 deposit you can apply for a bursary to cover the deposit, your travel and subsistence.

MASTER HMO'S TODAY,
CHANGE YOUR LIFE
FOREVER

HMO Mastery-Mentorship Programme - £667 pcm or £7,000 for full 12 months

Property training is a fantastic way to extend your knowledge and learn what to do and what not to do. But how many times have you attended a training day, got home full of good intentions to change your world, only to lose momentum the following day, week, month?

To keep you focused and continually moving forwards in your journey, HMO Daddy has carefully crafted the 12-month Mastery Programme which will provide you with on-going training, coaching and support for the next 12 months of your property journey.

The Mastery Programme is designed to encourage you to think outside of your natural capabilities. It will push you to the next level and most importantly the programme will keep you accountable in both a group setting and individually.

During each monthly session, held 1-4pm at our Wednesbury office on the first Tuesday of the month excluding August and December, you will work to develop your business and goals, you will analyse your deals and discuss your challenges with the HMO Daddy team and the other Mastery members. We will then review your activity every month so the grass never grows under your feet and you can be accountable for your own progress. You can ask questions to people that have already done what you are thinking of doing, which will help you to make the right choices to achieve the best results.

The first step of our Mastery Programme is a one-to-one session with Jim Haliburton to plan your 12-month journey and set goals to get you started. He will be able to keep things realistic and he will push you to think creatively and break through your own ceiling.

In addition to these interactive sessions, you have access to unlimited deal analysis with the HMO Daddy team. You can call the team at any time for advice and help and 'crunch the numbers' and you will receive our exclusive spreadsheet that allows you to analyse your own deals at any time. You also have unlimited access to the HMO Daddy team any time you need advice or support throughout your 12-month journey.

As if all of that was not enough, all of our Mastery members also get the following for no extra charge:

- The HMO Daddy Business in A Bag – 4 operational manuals to set up your HMO business – cost £1,395

- 6 books authored by Jim Haliburton – cost £54.55

- Entry to all of the HMO Daddy courses throughout the 12 months – FOC – costs over £5,000

- Inner Circle Membership – Facebook community and monthly tips and tricks and all webcasts

- Option to spend 3 full days in the J9 lettings part of the business to learn the intricacies of this business – cost £795

- First refusal on JV deals

- Access to the HMO Daddy Power Team - legal, financial, maintenance – priceless

One-to-One Consultations – phone or face-to-face

Telephone or face-to-face consultation. Are you too busy or not inclined to attend a course or just don't know where to start? Then you can have a one-to-one consultation with HMO Daddy or one of HMO Daddy's consultants.

With HMO Daddy	With HMO Daddy's Consultant
½ Hour Fee - **£150**	½ Hour Fee - **£75**
1 Hour Fee - **£250**	1 Hour Fee - **£125**
Half-Day Fee - **£800**	Half-Day Fee - **£400**
Full-Day Fee - **£1400**	Full-Day Fee - **£700**